ROYAL GARDENS

For Mr and Mrs Webster.

With best wishes.
George Plumptre.
October 1981.

ROYAL GARDENS

GEORGE PLUMPTRE

with photographs by

DERRY MOORE

COLLINS
St James's Place, London
1981

Frontispiece: The Savill Gardens, Windsor Great Park

All of the previously published extracts from the Royal Archives whose sources are listed below have been published by gracious permission of Her Majesty the Queen.

These are signified in the text by superior figures.

SANDRINGHAM: 1. *Sandringham.* Helen Cathcart. (London 1964).

ROYAL LODGE: 1. *King George VI.* John Wheeler-Bennett. (London 1958).

FROGMORE: 1, 2, 3, 4. *Queen Charlotte.* Olwyn Hedley. (London 1975).

BALMORAL: 1, 2, 3. *Victoria in The Highlands.* David Duff. (London 1968); 4. *Queen Mary.* James Pope-Hennessy. (London 1959); 5. Royal Archives GV CC4/246; 6. Royal Archives GV CC4/249; 7. *King George V.* John Gore. (London 1941).

William Collins Sons and Co Ltd
London · Glasgow · Sydney · Auckland
Toronto · Johannesburg

Plumptre, George
Royal gardens.
1. Gardens – Great Britain
2. Palaces – Great Britain
I. Title
II. Moore, Derry
712'.7'0941   SB466.G7.R/
ISBN 0-00-211871-8

First published 1981
© text George Plumptre 1981
© photographs Derry Moore 1981
Photoset in Ehrhardt
by MS Filmsetting Ltd, Frome, Somerset
Made and Printed in Italy by
New Interlitho, SpA, Milan

CONTENTS

ACKNOWLEDGEMENTS

I would like to acknowledge the gracious permission of Her Majesty the Queen for the gardens of Windsor Castle, Sandringham, Frogmore and Balmoral to be open to the public at certain times, which enabled Derry Moore and myself to have access to them. The photographs of the Buckingham Palace gardens and the drawings on pages 53, 117, 158, 171, 174, 175 and 179 appear by the permission of Her Majesty the Queen. It was by gracious permission of Her Majesty Queen Elizabeth the Queen Mother that Derry Moore and myself were able to visit and photograph the gardens at the Royal Lodge, Birkhall and the Castle of Mey, and by kind permission of Her Royal Highness Princess Alice, Duchess of Gloucester, that we were able to do the same at Barnwell Manor, for which I would also like to show my gratitude. The illustrations on pages 139 and 165 were reproduced by permission of the Trustees of the Sir John Soane Museum, and the illustration on page 172 was reproduced by permission of the British Library. I received considerable help over the preparation of the book from various members of Her Majesty the Queen's Household at Buckingham Palace, the Lord Chamberlain's Office and at Windsor Castle, as well as from members of Her Majesty Queen Elizabeth the Queen Mother's Household at Clarence House, and Her Royal Highness Princess Alice, Duchess of Gloucester's Household at Kensington Palace. Equally, when visiting the gardens during 1980, I received continual help and advice from a number of members of the Estate Offices at Sandringham, Balmoral, Birkhall, the Castle of Mey, Barnwell and the Royal Lodge. I must also thank members of the Department of the Environment for help over Hampton Court gardens, and members of the Crown Estate Commissioners for help over the gardens in Windsor Great Park.

During the months of research, both into the history and about the gardens as they are today, many people gave invaluable help in different ways, for which I am very grateful. I was lucky enough to have a number of conversations with the late Sir Eric Savill during the early stages of preparation, when he gave me kind and very relevant advice. Generous help and useful information came from Hope Findlay about the Savill Gardens, the Royal Lodge and Sandringham; from Lord Adam Gordon about Birkhall and the Castle of Mey; from Sir Geoffrey Jellicoe about the Royal Lodge and Sandringham; from Tom Lichfield and Nicholas Warliker about Barnwell; from George Cooke about Hampton Court; from John Bond and Andrew Jackson about the gardens in Windsor Great Park; from Peter Coats about Buckingham Palace; and from Lanning Roper about the Savill Gardens. I must thank the last two especially for generously allowing me to refer to their respective books about the Buckingham Palace gardens and the Savill Gardens. For advice not specifically about any single one of the gardens but which greatly helped the book's general progress, I must thank Sir Hugh Casson, Alan Hardy, Major Raymond Seymour, Hugo Vickers and, especially, Hugh Montgomery-Massingberd. Finally, I must thank my agent Vivienne Schuster, my editor Robin Baird-Smith, and Gill Gibbins and Vera Brice at Collins Publishers, as well as my mother and a number of friends, whose continual encouragement was both reassuring and a source of strength. Of course my greatest debt, which it would be difficult to repay, is to Derry Moore, not only for his photographs but also for making *Royal Gardens* such an enjoyable partnership.

Goodnestone. July 1981

INTRODUCTION

THE RELATIONSHIP BETWEEN the Monarchy and gardens through English history is an eventful, varied and often spectacular story. There is perhaps no other body whose gardens have, over the centuries, contained such diversity of conception, style and situation, and which together give such a revealing insight into the development of gardens in this country. There is also no doubt that the Royal contribution to horticulture and garden history has been quite remarkable, comparable to, if not on the same scale as their building projects and the unique contribution their collections of works of art have made to the national heritage. Added to this is the idea of envisaging gardens through Royal eyes: how they planned them during different periods, who they employed and what they were trying to create. The chapters which follow describe the background and appearance of the gardens around eleven of the main Royal homes and residences of today (apart from the Savill Gardens, which are not laid out around a house but are part of the Royal domain of Windsor Park); they also attempt to illustrate the theme of continuity and contrast which these gardens contain. The history of the Royal gardens dates from the feudal Middle Ages when, with monastic gardens, they were among the only gardens in England; through the glorious zenith of the late seventeenth and early eighteenth centuries to the present day.

It was largely King George VI who prompted the landscape-architect Sir Geoffrey Jellicoe's ideas on what he was later to call the psychology of landscape, when the latter was advising the King on the gardens at the Royal Lodge. This psychology – the ambitions and aspirations behind the creations – is inherent in the Royal gardens. In some cases it was a search for grandeur – often stimulated by competition: Henry VIII was determined to outdo Cardinal Wolsey's achievements at Hampton Court, and both Charles II (with his gardens at St James's Palace and Greenwich Palace, as well as at Hampton Court) and William III had visions of excelling Louis XIV's vast and legendary palace at Versailles; while George IV's work at Buckingham Palace and Windsor Castle was inspired by the limitless extent, combined with outstanding taste, of his own ambitions and ideas.

These were all cases of Royal patronage on the grand scale where the monarchs were trying to create a visible embodiment of their power and wealth, at the same time as indulging their artistic taste. Equally illustrative of the unceasing part played by Royal patronage were Queen Charlotte's creation of the gardens at Frogmore, King Edward VII's lavish expenditure in making Sandringham the epitome of Edwardianism and the later sympathetic adoption of the gardens there by King George VI and Queen Elizabeth. In recent years the Queen Mother's rescue of the Castle of Mey is a striking example of the will to restore and create.

Perhaps most recurrent, particularly since the Victorian era, has been the continual quest for privacy. A desire for privacy is by no means limited to this later period – it was fundamental to the medieval gardens at Windsor Castle, as indeed it was to Queen Elizabeth I's enjoyment of Hampton Court and to Queen Charlotte's world of Frogmore. But it is since Queen Victoria's reign, when the distinction between public and private life has become increasingly more important (if more difficult to achieve) to members of the Royal Family, that it has had the most obvious effect on their homes and gardens. For Queen Victoria and Prince Albert Balmoral (and equally Osborne) was somewhere where they could enjoy their private life away from the pressures of political and court life in London and at Windsor. During Queen Victoria's widowhood the gardens of Buckingham Palace and Frogmore were seemingly barricaded by dense evergreen shrubberies. Edward VII may have enjoyed continually entertaining on a lavish scale at Sandringham, but it was always on the premise that it was his private home and estate; for his wife, Queen Alexandra, Sandringham was always home, where she could enjoy relaxation and peace – whether among the quantities of personal bric-a-brac with which she filled the house, or in the little garden around her dairy. The urge for a truly private world is clearly shown in the work of King George VI and Queen Elizabeth at the Royal Lodge and in their commissioning of the enclosed north garden at Sandringham. The achievement of this privacy is the basis of the Royal Family's stays at any of their homes, be it Sandringham, Balmoral or Birkhall, Barnwell or Mey. It has, however, been simultaneous with the highly commendable decision to allow public access to some of their gardens. Queen Victoria started the trend by opening the grounds of Hampton Court in 1838. Now the grounds of Sandringham and Balmoral are open during much of the summer, the public have access to part of the Windsor Castle gardens, and, on limited days, to Frogmore and Barnwell. The Savill Gardens were always intended to be fully accessible to the public.

Through the years a great variety of characters have influenced the gardens in different ways, ranging from Henry II to the present generations of the Royal Family; and it is true to say that, with only one or two exceptions, every monarch since Henry VIII has left some mark in one or more of the gardens discussed. As well as the monarchs, there is the illustrious group of men who were employed at various times to execute the work, and in many cases to enhance the landscape with their undisputed genius: John Tradescant II, John Rose, George London and Henry Wise, André le Nôtre, Jean Tijou, William Talman, 'Capability' Brown, William Aiton, Jeffrey Wyatville, Eric Savill, Geoffrey Jellicoe and others. However, all the Royal gardens have one notable feature in common – the harmony between the style of the gardens and the character of their surroundings, something as evident at Birkhall among the wooded hills of Deeside as it is at the Royal Lodge in the heart of Windsor Great Park.

One of the greatest influences has been Victorianism. Today The Queen is as conscious of Queen Victoria's personality and achievements as was her grandfather King George V; and they are to be felt and seen in most of the Royal gardens. The influence is naturally strongest at the homes and residences which Queen Victoria used: Windsor Castle and Frogmore, Balmoral and Birkhall, while the Edwardianism of Sandringham was, in a sense, the extravagant swan-song of the Victorian era. One of the gardens' most notable features, their superb trees, results from a practice started by Queen Victoria of commemorative planting, which has been avidly continued by subsequent generations of the Royal Family. The trees, many now in splendid maturity, not only signpost the private and public events of Royal life but, by the inscriptions on their inevitable plaques, reveal the size of Queen Victoria's family – for the European relations it was virtually compulsory to plant an oak, fir, beech or cedar whenever they visited England.

In more recent times it has been the Queen Mother who has played the leading role in the shaping of Royal gardens. Both she and King George VI were talented and knowledgeable gardeners, (and in one or two cases their work has succeeded in enhancing a somewhat gloomy appearance surviving from the nineteenth century). The Queen Mother's enthusiasm in particular has left its mark in the gardens of all her homes, but it is at the Royal Lodge, Birkhall and the Castle of Mey that her achievements are most evident.

Unfortunately, the Royal Family do not always have time or are rarely in one place for long enough to be able to devote the attention necessary for adventurous innovation in their gardens and in the circumstances continuity and careful improvement are the safer course. Their gardens do, however, indisputably contain features of unrivalled quality and beauty, and they have a special interest because of the interplay of their individual characters with the general world in which they have evolved. They are intriguing because they abound with a sense of history – indeed, they are part of our history – and because they clearly reflect Royal tastes, past and present.

SANDRINGHAM

Norfolk

WHEN THE PRINCE OF WALES first visited Sandringham in February 1862 with members of his household, he was not put off by the drab exterior of the house or by any of the shortcomings he came across when going round the estate. No doubt memories of his father's wishes, who had died only two months previously, filled his mind, and the Prince of Wales left Sandringham determined that it would become his country home. Thus it was that by the autumn of 1862 he had purchased an estate described by neighbouring contemporaries as, 'wind-swept, barren, sandy moorland', and 'the wildest and most out-of-the-way place imaginable'; one of whose farms appeared to a new tenant as, 'a scene of dirt, ruin and desolation'. It was no coincidence that the estate belonged to the Hon. Charles Spencer Cowper, Lord Palmerston's stepson (Palmerston having married his mother Emmy, widow of Earl Cowper in 1839). By setting up the sale Palmerston showed neat adroitness in overcoming the suspicion and dislike which both Queen Victoria and the Prince Consort had shown towards him, as well as financially guaranteeing his stepson's future. £220,000 was paid for an estate of just under eight thousand acres and an unprepossessing Georgian house rendered in stucco. But over the last hundred and twenty years the expense would appear to have justified itself. Clearly distinct from the various Royal residences, Sandringham is the Royal Family's own country home and as such commands a special affection.

Ever since the present Sandringham House was built the relation between the house and the gardens around it has been of fundamental importance. Both are of formidable size, and as a result the gardens have been able to mellow the effect of the enormous and not immediately

Opposite: Sandringham, the supreme Edwardian country house

Overleaf: Looking from the Dell across the upper pond, with the huge trees and lawns of the gardens towards York Cottage in the background

attractive house with a suitably spacious setting on every side. In his biography *Queen Mary* James Pope-Hennessy expresses the opinion that the gardens are the saving grace at Sandringham and make up for the architectural shortcomings of the house. But it should be added that since then the gardens have lost many of their late-Victorian features, such as the formal flower parterre, the rosery and the maze, and now Sandringham can surely be seen as a supreme product of its Edwardian age, possessing as such an individual, if unconventional, charm. The scale on which everything was done reflected the Edwardian age in which the new home was conceived and in particular it reflected the character of the man who was the *prima mobilis* of Edwardianism, the Prince of Wales. The development of the house, gardens and estate went hand-in-hand as it has done, with changes in policy and priorities, ever since; for at Sandringham the Royal Family have been able to care for and administer their property as many other landowners do all over Britain, free from the feeling that they are life-tenants of the State.

The house, which was then called Sandringham Hall, had been built by Cornish Hoste Henley and completed in 1771. Henley had come to Sandringham when he married Susan Hoste, the heiress of the estate, whose family had owned it since 1686. Despite his wife's fortune and the example of his neighbours, Holkham and Houghton, Henley's house was not architecturally inspired; and although he took an interest in the estate and improved the farming and the woodlands he does not seem to have held any strong ambition to improve the landscape which surrounded the new house. His son, Henry Hoste Henley, had four children, none of whom survived him, and therefore after his death in 1833 the estate, then only 5450 acres, was put up for auction and bought in 1836 (for £76,000) by John Motteux, who was descended from a Huguenot refugee.

By the 1820s Motteux had achieved considerable wealth and social success, in particular a firm friendship with the Earl and Countess Cowper, Charles Spencer Cowpers' parents. Among his other qualities Motteux was a keen horticulturalist and a specialist in the cultivation of pears. In 1826 he won the Large Silver Medal of the Horticultural Society for his pears, and in 1831 Talleyrand was reputed to have inquired at a dinner-party in Paris, 'and who is this little man *with his mania for pears*?' The fact that Motteux was unmarried led him to take an avuncular interest in the lives of the Cowpers' children; it is quite likely that the idea of leaving his inheritance to one of them influenced his decision when he was considering investing in Sandringham. The property was already well-known to him as his own estate of Beachamwell lay close by to the south-east of King's Lynn. Motteux was dealt two blows shortly after his purchase of Sandringham by the deaths of his only brother Robert and of Lord Cowper; possibly as a result he never lived at Sandringham, being content to add well over 1000 acres to the estate. It was perhaps the logical conclusion of his ambitions that on his death in 1843 Motteux's will

named Charles Spencer Cowper, who had always been his favourite, as the heir to his Norfolk properties.

In 1852 Cowper married Harriet, Countess d'Orsay, widow of the notorious Count Alfred d'Orsay. Harriet had married d'Orsay at the age of fifteen, and although the marriage was an unqualified failure – doubtless because d'Orsay was having an affair with Harriet's widowed mother, the Countess of Blessington, in a scandalous *mènage à trois* – she was unable to re-marry until his death. Cowper's arrival at Sandringham with his pregnant wife in 1852 heralded the alterations which were to give the house an incongruous, almost bizarre appearance, but which bestowed a great deal of favour on Sandringham in the young Prince of Wales's eyes. Cowper commissioned Samuel Sanders Teulon, a fashionable disciple of High-Victorian Gothic architecture, to make certain improvements to the house including a conservatory of carstone and brick, a bay-window below the central gable on the garden front and a balustrade around the terrace on that side, as well as tall, brick Tudor-style chimneys to stop the fires smoking. On the entrance front Teulon added an ornate two-storey porch of white and red brickwork, which to an unfavourable eye must have suggested something akin to the false nose protruding from the chalky face of a clown.

After his purchase of the estate had been completed the Prince of Wales wasted no time in embarking on alterations and improvements at Sandringham. While at Balmoral in 1862 he persuaded the head gardener to travel south to Norfolk and give advice towards planning the Sandringham gardens. Far more important for the future of Sandringham was the marriage of the Prince of Wales to Princess Alexandra of Denmark in March 1863, for in the next two or three years the prospect of a growing family and large numbers of guests made it increasingly obvious that whatever improvements might be made to the house it was not large enough for the Prince of Wales's needs. A sentimental attachment to the old house meant that the Prince's architect, Albert Jenkins Humbert, was stretched to the limits of his powers in his attempts to accommodate the Prince's wishes with what was practicable.

At first the Prince was adamant about retaining all of Teulon's various embellishments, having been guided to show great admiration for his work by one of the architect's patrons, the Duke of St Albans. Humbert was asked to plan alterations to the house which retained the old chimney-stacks, a virtually impossible task; and the Prince only agreed to the replacement of the porch with a larger, less startling one when he realized that his guests were getting wet when they arrived. But by the Christmas of 1866, when the house was overcrowded and Princess Alexandra was driven back to London early suffering terrible rheumatism caused by the damp, the Prince of Wales began to give in. After rejecting Humbert's first two or three proposals for a new house he agreed to a new set of designs,

and the way was open for the old house to be demolished and rebuilt, which took from 1868 to 1870.

Shortly after the Prince of Wales's marriage the gardens gained the impressive addition of the Norwich Gates. The gates had been made by Thomas Jekyll of Norwich and were on show at the Great Exhibition of 1862, after which they were presented to the Prince and Princess of Wales as a wedding present from the county of Norfolk. The huge wrought-iron

Redwoods close to York Cottage; fine examples of Sandringham's outstanding trees planted unceasingly by generations of the Royal Family

panels of intricate floral patterns were placed at the main entrance to the grounds and opened on to the lime avenue – possibly planted by Motteux – which led straight to the north front of the house. They were joined by four pillars, each surmounted with griffins holding shields emblazoned with the arms of the Prince's various titles, with the Royal arms and crown in the centre. To accommodate the majestic gates a new wall was built around the gardens.

In the early years of Royal Sandringham, during the 1860s, there were few major changes to the gardens, but one other addition was a semi-circular house for camellias, designed by Humbert, which bore out the contemporary belief that camellias were too vulnerable to winter out-of-doors. And in 1865 an entry in the diary of the Prince of Wales's friend, Admiral Sir Henry Keppel, shows how the Prince seemed to be perpetuating the interest in fruit trees which Motteux brought to Sandringham: 'Prince and self planted first apple and pear trees in new kitchen garden.'

The completion of Humbert's new house, which was ready just in time for the Prince's birthday in 1870, was by contrast accompanied by sweeping changes in the gardens. W. B. Thomas, the garden designer who incurred Queen Victoria's wrath by trying to clear some of the shrubberies in the Buckingham Palace gardens, was called in to plan new lay-outs, and the result was an almost total transformation on the west front of the house. Because the new house was positioned further to the east than the old one, the terrace along the west front covered ground which had been part of the interior. Below the terrace the lake, which had been positioned uncomfortably close to the house, was filled in; in its place appeared a large colourful parterre of flower-beds so typical of mid-Victorian gardens, with small trees of clipped golden holly and yew breaking the horizontal flatness of the pattern. Beyond the parterre to the south-west Thomas excavated two new lakes. The lower lake, which in later years would be looked on to by the Bachelors' or York Cottage, was made round a large island, while flowing into the top corner of the upper lake was the little stream and valley which became the Dell. Opposite the Dell, James Pulham, well known for his rock and water gardens, was employed to build a rockery, and the boathouse, or Grotto, out of local carstone.

One of the first ornaments brought to the gardens was the Chinese Joss, who was placed to the north of the house looking down the terrace stretching along the west front. The Joss represents the Buddhist divinity Kuvera and was a gift from Admiral Keppel, whom the Prince of Wales had helped gain the command of the China and Japan station in 1866. Keppel brought the splendid brass figure from China and it arrived at Sandringham in April 1870 to await the arrival of the Prince of Wales later in the year for his birthday. While the Joss was being put in position it was discovered that its hollow interior contained a number of coins inserted –

The Joss, no longer
protected by his pagoda,
but continuing to sit as he
has done for over a
hundred years

obviously – for luck, as the inscription on the outside reads, 'Respectfully
made on a lucky day of the tenth month of the twenty-eighth year of His
Majesty K'-ang-Hsi. (October or November 1690).' Soon after the Joss's
arrival the Prince ordered a small pagoda to be made to house the figure
which then sat gazing blandly towards the house, flanked by two Japanese
stone dogs.

The parterre, lakes and Joss were all blended into the wider setting by
the stretches of lawn, planted with trees either in groups or singly, which
surrounded the house. The older specimens were continuously added to,
the new trees often being planted by cousins from various European
families to mark the occasion of a visit to Sandringham, a fact always
dutifully recorded on a plaque by each tree. After the completion of the
new house the Prince of Wales's life at Sandringham took on a steadily
developing pattern divided between unceasing involvement in maintaining and improving his estate and the entertainment of his increasing
numbers of guests. Disraeli, who was a regular visitor, shows how the two
were often combined, and how as well as shooting and the indoor
activities, a regular part of a visit to Sandringham was accompanying the

Prince to visit a new cottage, farm or cow, or part of the gardens. 'He is really fond of this place, is making endless improvements in his grounds ... Then we are building cottages on a new plan which I should think was our own, for we are very fond of it; and we have prize beasts and patent sheep and all that sort of thing ... We had to go over 14 acres of *jardin potager*, and visit royal farms and dairies. The glass houses are striking; one of them containing a grove of banana trees weighed down with clustering fruit, remarkable; and a parrot house of the Princess's with great variety of birds of that species, noisy but amusing ...' It would seem that the grounds of Sandringham became something of a zoo in the same way as those of Buckingham Palace, for as well as the parrots there were other creatures, including two bears and some monkeys.

Princess Alexandra's life at Sandringham was far more relaxed than her husband's, and she was often to be found sorting through or adding to her enormous collections of knick-knacks, bric-à-brac and photographs which gave some of Sandringham's rooms the appearance of an over-crowded antique shop, where a visitor worried about sitting down in case he crushed some unseen little object. For the Princess the whole world of Sandringham was such a delight that she was usually happy to enjoy it as it was, without wishing to involve herself in her husband's numerous projects. She was quite content walking or sitting in the gardens or driving around the countryside in her pony and trap.

By the 1880s it was becoming clear that the house was still not large enough for the scale of the Prince of Wales's entertainments, the balls and shooting parties for large numbers of guests. In 1881 he engaged a new architect, Colonel Robert Edis, to build a square wing on to the south-eastern side of the house which would contain a new ballroom and, among the other rooms, a large conservatory, making up for the loss of Teulon's saved from the old house but converted into a billiard room. Adjoining the old conservatory was one of the Prince's favourite additions, a bowling-alley, which he built after a visit to the Duke of Sutherland's seat at Trentham in Staffordshire where he had been impressed by such a novelty.

Edis's extensions to the house were completed in time for the ill-fated Duke of Clarence's coming-of-age celebrations in 1885 and, more important, for Queen Victoria's second and last visit to Sandringham in 1889. As was to be expected, Queen Victoria marked the visit by planting a tree, an oak positioned prominently on the lawn in front of the main entrance. Her Majesty duly recorded the occasion in her diary; 'Out with Bertie [the Prince of Wales] and Alix [the Princess of Wales], Louise [their eldest daughter] and all the children, and I planted a tree in front of the house.' By the 1890s, however, Sandringham's steady ascent to a peak of country-house life suffered two setbacks. The first, a fire which broke out in the top of the house in October 1891, has sometimes been seen as a blessing in disguise, for the damage was not as extensive as originally

Queen Alexandra's Dairy Garden, in its heyday before the First World War

Overleaf: The gates given to King Edward VII in 1905 by the Prince and Princess of Wales (King George V and Queen Mary), which open on to the enormous pergola

feared, and as a result Edis added a wing over the billiard room and bowling alley which greatly enhanced the appearance of the west front. Far more tragic, in 1892, was the death of the Duke of Clarence at the age of twenty-eight from the shock of which neither the Prince nor, more especially, the Princess of Wales ever really recovered.

The sadness of the Duke of Clarence's death was partially dispelled by the marriage in 1893 of his fiancée, Princess May of Teck, to his own younger brother, the Duke of York (later King George V). The couple took over York Cottage (as the Bachelors' Cottage was now known), despite the house's limited size and less than enchanting appearance. Sir Harold Nicolson described it in his biography *King George V* as, 'a glum little villa, encompassed by thickets of laurel and rhododendron, shadowed by huge Wellingtonias and separated by an abrupt rim of lawn from a pond, at the edge of which a leaden pelican gazes in dejection upon the water lilies and bamboos.'

With the Yorks installed at York Cottage, life at Sandringham took a happier turn and continued toward the zenith which the house was to enjoy around the turn of the century and in the years of the Prince's eventual reign. The triumphs of his most famous horse, Persimmon (who

won the Derby, the St Leger and the Jockey Club Stakes in 1896 and the Eclipse Stakes and the Gold Cup in 1897) led him to joke that the horse was financing the Sandringham gardens. To a certain extent this was true, for along the north side of the walled gardens, which lay across the Hillington road from the east front of the house, a huge range of teak greenhouses was built with some of the winnings and suitably named the Persimmon range. Another new addition was the rosery where in June the rose-beds and surrounding metal bowers, draped in climbing roses, were a mass of bloom surrounding a central fountain and statue. The rosery was made on the site of an old bowling-green; its summer-house had originally been a pavilion, and was a favourite place for the Prince of Wales to take his guests for a walk in summer.

If the Prince of Wales enjoyed accompanying his guests at an energetic pace amongst the rose borders or, best of all, to view the splendours of the Persimmon range, one of the Princess of Wales's favourite haunts was the little garden around the Dairy which had been built for her in a corner of the walled gardens. The Dairy was modelled on Queen Victoria's Swiss Cottage at Osborne – also owing something perhaps to the influence of Marie Antoinette – and many of the Princess's guests were entertained to tea there, looking out on to the topiary-work which filled the surrounding garden. For the children at York Cottage one of the main delights of the gardens must have been the nearby maze, amongst whose box and yew hedges they could spend hours happily getting lost and finding themselves again.

Although the Prince of Wales's visits to Sandringham were necessarily reduced when he acceded to the throne in 1901 it continued to demand his energetic and often overpowering attention. Intrinsic in his life were the endless series of schemes with which he busied himself – the improvement of the estate, or some part of the house; plans for a golf-course in the park or to replace the bowling-alley with a library; and of course, schemes for the gardens. After he had become King, Edward VII remarked to Admiral 'Jacky' Fisher that if he could have chosen his own career he would have become a landscape gardener – a seemingly uncharacteristic choice in view of his love of the fleshpots, but a theory it is possible to believe in the context of Sandringham. While new trees continued to appear on the lawns around the house during King Edward VII's reign, major projects were going ahead in the east gardens over the road, at the end of which their size and level of cultivation could possibly have been supported only in a period of such affluence as the Edwardian age.

In 1905 the new Prince and Princess of Wales presented the King with a magnificent pair of wrought-iron gates, set between brick piers surmounted by stone urns, which were placed at the entrance to the east gardens, opposite the small wooden door in the wall of the main gardens around the house. At the same time the pergola, which is one of the outstanding features of the Sandringham gardens and the longest in

England, was erected to lead from them, between the lawns and flower-beds on either side, to the main area of the east gardens along the north side of which stretched the Persimmon range. The pergola is 70 yards long and built on a cube pattern, the height, width and distance between each of the brick piers being 15 feet. Covering the brick columns is the pergola-pattern of oak beams which, after the construction was finished, were soon draped in numerous climbing plants. In 1912 the head gardener at Sandringham gave an account of the kitchen (east) gardens, showing the amount of attention they required, almost inconceivable today: 'The Kitchen Garden (some 16 acres in extent) is divided by a wide central walk 310 yards long and 12 feet wide, with broad herbaceous and mixed flower borders on both sides, which from early spring to November present an endless variety of hardy flowering plants. The edging is of Staffordshire brick, which is hidden in summer by low-growing alpines and bright annuals breaking the hardness of the straight edges and extending over the pathway. For background there is a high fence of Cordon Apple trees, with iron arches (set lengthways) also covered with trained apples. They present a beautiful sight in blossom time, and again when hung with rosy or golden fruit. The central walk is bisected by another running north and south, with rose borders on either side, and high arched fences of climbing roses behind. Where these walks cross in the centre of the garden there is a beautiful large fountain and circular basin in red marble. It is surrounded some 14 feet away with rose-covered arches. At the east end of the central walk two borders of Tritomas and Michaelmas daisies are a pleasing feature; and in the wall beyond (leading to the pink Hermosa Rose walk), is a beautiful wrought-iron gilded gate, the design of which is a grape vine bearing fruit. A high fence 90 yards long (covered with Dorothy Perkins roses), dividing the Hermosa Rose walk from vegetable ground behind, is,

Faded grandeur: in the old east gardens the disused fountain and a pair of gates, surmounted by the crown and Edward and Alexandra's intertwined monograms

when in flower, one of the most admired objects in the garden. By way of contrast, 7-feet high standards of crimson Hiawatha have been planted at intervals among the Hermosas, and as edging the charming little Polyantha Rose – Jessie, is used.' When considering that all these flower borders and avenues of fruit trees hid rows of vegetables, in addition to which a rose fence 300 yards long stretched the length of the path in front of the Persimmon glasshouses, and trained fruit trees covered the brick walls surrounding the garden, it is understandable that in 1906 there were ninety-one gardeners at Sandringham to look after these east gardens and those around the house itself.

In 1908, as a result of a terrific gale, Sandringham lost one of the best-known features of its gardens which pre-dated the Royal occupation of the house – the stately lime avenue which led from the Norwich Gates to the north front of the house. The gale all but destroyed the avenue and it was decided to fell those trees which survived because of their age and not to fill in the enormous gaps; as a result the north front of the house was exposed to view from the Dersingham road. After a proposal to move the Norwich Gates and make an entrance in the wall to the east of the house was firmly rejected by Queen Alexandra, a far more costly solution was decided upon. The gates were removed to a position 160 yards further to the north of the house, the public road diverted and the perimeter wall extended accordingly to take in a strip of the adjacent Dersingham woods, now called the Glade, whose trees would once again ensure the privacy of the house. It was not long before quantities of daffodils were planted in the grass below the Scots Pines and other trees of the Glade, as well as a number of flowering and ornamental trees and shrubs.

By the time of King Edward VII's death in 1910 Sandringham had grown to monumental proportions in almost every aspect. The house contained 365 rooms, more than any other private house in England, then or now. In the half-century that he lived there Edward VII gave Sandringham a powerful aura which it has never lost during the subsequent decline from the pinnacle of country-house life which it had achieved. During the First World War, which followed four years after his death, the flower-beds of the east gardens were replaced by more rows of vegetables and the lavishness of the pre-war years was never attained again.

After King Edward VII's death Queen Alexandra spent most of her time at Sandringham, living with her devoted lady-in-waiting Charlotte Knollys, and Comptroller-General, Sir Dighton Probyn, in the huge house which had always been her favourite home. In 1913 Probyn made a gift to Queen Alexandra of the little summer-house which stands screened by dwarf conifers and evergreen bushes on the rockery over the grotto beside the upper lake. Probyn called the summer-house 'The Nest' and showed his affection for Queen Alexandra, whom he called 'The Blessed Lady', with an inscription on the inside: 'The Queen's Nest – A small

Overleaf: The Norwich Gates, with Dersingham Woods bounding the gardens. Where the huge lime avenue once led to the north front of the house the drive is now flanked by rhododendrons

offering to The Blessed Lady from Her Beloved Majesty's very devoted old servant General Probyn, 1913 – Today tomorrow and every day God bless and guard her I fervently pray.' From the summer-house Queen Alexandra could look across the water lilies and little island at the top of the upper lake to the Dell on the far side, which had always been one of her favourite parts of the gardens.

The gardens of Sandringham House were first opened to the public in 1908, and the number of visitors has swelled each year ever since. In the summer of 1924 Cecil Beaton, then aged twenty, visited the gardens with his family. The highlight of the visit was seeing Queen Alexandra, an old lady of eighty and still retaining signs of the beauty which had endeared her to so many people. He recorded in his diary his impression of the gardens, which struck him as an uninspired product of an age they had outlived: 'The Royal gardens, in spite of an impressive orderliness and formality, showed no imagination. It was only near the house, in contrast to the red brick, that the mass of ramblers and yellow privet hedges acquired a solid Victorian charm.'

A year later Queen Alexandra was dead and the last direct tie with the Edwardianism in which Sandringham had been conceived was gone. There were no sweeping changes, though, when King George V and Queen Mary moved into the 'Big House' from York Cottage. For the King, Sandringham was as it always had been – 'dear old Sandringham, the place I love better than anywhere else in the world'. He was far too sensitive to it having been his parents' home and of their continuing influence to want to change anything that was not absolutely necessary. Queen Mary had always been very fond of the gardens, and when the Prince of Wales (later King Edward VIII) made a visit in the summer of 1926 she wrote that, 'He was simply enchanted with Sandringham in the summer and with the lovely flower-beds in front of the house. I don't think that he has ever been here in the summer since he was a child.'[1] The one exception to Queen Mary's approval, as at all the other Royal homes where it reared its ugly head, was ivy, and where it grew on the walls of the house she immediately organized its removal, and suggested it be replaced with a wisteria.

The death of King George V in 1936 marked the end of the old order at Sandringham, as the end of the Second World War marked the beginning of fundamental changes in the gardens, revealing the emergence of different styles and orders of priority. In his short reign King Edward VIII had put an end to 'Sandringham Time' – initiated by King Edward VII when he was Prince of Wales – whereby all the clocks were permanently half an hour fast to extend shooting days, (supposedly saying, 'I'll fix those bloody clocks'); and had ordered a complete survey of the estate by his brother the Duke of York (later King

Previous page: Typical East Anglian landscape: low horizons and vast skies. Open parkland, framed by oak and copper beech, stretches away from York Cottage Lake

One of the thatched summer houses built by George VI in the old kitchen gardens

George VI), to see where possible economies could be made. King George VI was far more of a traditionalist than his brother, but both he and Queen Elizabeth were talented and enthusiastic gardeners. The alterations which appeared at Sandringham reflected their personal desires as well as the need for labour-saving economies.

In the post-war world, when so much of Royal life was not only taken up with official duties but also increasingly, and at times oppressively, public, the King and Queen Elizabeth treasured the aspects of their private life more and more. As a result, in 1947 Geoffrey Jellicoe, who had already extensively re-planned parts of the Royal Lodge gardens, was asked by the King to design and lay out a garden extending away from the north front of the house where the private apartments were. The drive was diverted to curve round to the main entrance on the east front; and a belt of shrubbery and woodland which screened the top of the north garden, extending to an old stand of Scots Pines, at least ensured that the house was no longer visible from the Norwich Gates. The dominant aim of Jellicoe's north garden was to fulfil the desire for privacy and to provide the King and Queen Elizabeth with a personal, intimate garden in the midst of the sweeping lawns and stately trees. As at the Royal Lodge, Jellicoe found that he was not so much working for the King as working with him. 'King George knew precisely what he wanted in landscapes,' said Jellicoe. 'Though he was not always familiar with the technique of getting it, he was able to detect if the experts were moving on the wrong lines. Many of his instructions were accompanied by his own pencil notes, and these provided a basis of discussion on which the design would develop. He would pass constantly from drawings to the site and back again . . . and he took a hand in all setting out by the contractor, enjoying as much as anyone the rough and tumble of earthworks.'

The garden which emerged below the windows of the north front is a long rectangle filled with a formal pattern of intricately connected enclosures, each surrounded with hedges of box. In most of the enclosures mixed flower-beds, containing in particular, many roses for the benefit of Queen Elizabeth, are divided by trim grass and gravel paths; and in the middle of the garden, on either side of the long central grass path, are two secluded patches of box-enclosed lawn, designed for the Royal Family's tea parties in summer. The whole garden is flanked, save on the side closest to the house, by double avenues of pleached limes reminiscent of the old avenue destroyed in 1908. A melancholy statue of Father Time, bought by Queen Mary in 1950, gazes from the far end towards the house. The old boy is curiously juxtaposed with the Joss, who has not moved since he arrived at Sandringham over a hundred years ago, although he is no longer protected by his pagoda. Sadly the garden was too young before his death in 1952, for the King to enjoy to the full the seclusion he had planned, but today the box hedges have grown up, the branches of the lime avenues intertwine to form an arbour, and the garden clearly fulfis his aims.

By the time Jellicoe had completed the north garden, the main flower parterre on the east front and the smaller pansy garden in front of the guest wing had disappeared to be replaced by lawns. A number of the older trees had also been thinned from some of the roundels and shrubberies in the lawns – particularly on the east side of the house – and as a result the whole aspect of the house's surroundings was opened up. Instead of the time-consuming maintenance of the flower parterre, attention began to be focused on the area of the Glade and around the upper and lower lakes.

Since the 1950s these have become the part of the gardens of greatest visual interest, with increasing numbers of the plants of which the King and Queen Elizabeth were fond – rhododendrons, azaleas, magnolias and camellias – being planted in the woodland setting of the broad swathe of ground between the Dell and the Norwich Gates, and on round the perimeter wall. They formed new areas which both the Royal Family and visitors to the gardens could enjoy: paths winding among the woodland gardens along the northern perimeter, and the numerous vistas across the lawns and lakes. As a result, with the exception of the north garden, the gardens as a whole have assumed a more informal atmosphere and grown to contain an impressive variety of plants suited to the generally sandy soil.

Skilful planting around the mature standard trees has played a major part in the success of the Sandringham gardens in recent years. Standing between the upper and lower lakes a rich variety of views stretch away on every side. One can see past a magnificent oak tree, which is reputed to be eight hundred and fifty years old, towards the spreading trees and lawns to the south of the house; past the weeping birches and new rockery planted with dwarf conifers and heathers at the head of the lower lake to the mixed borders on the far bank, where among the colourful plants are irises, rhododendrons and agapanthus; across the upper lake to the rockery and ultimately to a glimpse of the house beyond; or to the Dell, which is highlighted in the spring by the flowers of a sixty-year old *Magnolia denudata* standing at the head of the little glade, and where new rhododendrons and azaleas among the older conifers form a backcloth to the numerous aquatic plants. A poignant reminder of the past is the Deodar cedar planted close to the Dell by King George V on 11 January 1936, only nine days before his death; between the Dell and the Glade to the north, the path trodden by generations of the Royal Family leads beneath an avenue of lofty Scots Pines between the house and Sandringham Church, which stands in the park.

One of the main qualities of the trees at Sandringham is their unbroken continuity of age resulting from the tradition of planting maintained by the Royal Family over the last hundred years. One of the most recent additions is an oak near the entrance to the Glade, planted by Queen Elizabeth II to mark her Silver Jubilee in 1977. Five years earlier in 1972, the Forestry Commission presented The Queen and Prince Philip with twenty-five trees to mark their Silver Wedding. The trees, which all have silver bark or foliage, include sorbus, ilex, eucalyptus, birch and spruce and have been planted beyond Queen Victoria's oak on the main east lawn.

As well as blending with the older trees the additions made to the gardens in recent years provide a wonderful variety of colour from the early spring until the autumn, particularly in the woodland garden which borders the wide grassy spaces of the Glade. Carpets of daffodils fill the gardens in early spring, covering the ground beneath the trees of the Glade

Opposite: Jellicoe's formal north garden flanked by avenues of pleached limes

Overleaf: Early morning at Sandringham; looking across one of the pleached lime avenues to the north-west corner of the house

or clustering in groups beside the lakes. A great feature of the woodland garden in early summer are the polyanthus which seem to be everywhere, filling the spaces between the rhododendrons, azaleas, camellias and other flowering shrubs – cornus, cotoneaster and philadelphus. The quantity of rhododendrons in the gardens is indicated by the fact that there are over two hundred varieties, flowering mainly in the spring and early summer but continuing until the superb white flowers of the hybrid 'Polar Bear' appear in July and August. Also adding to the array of early-summer colour in the woodland garden are many varieties of acers and magnolias, whose creamy-textured flowers – in species like *Magnolia obovata* – appear among exotically large leaves. Close to where the woodland garden reaches the Norwich Gates stands a large specimen of *Davidia involucrata*, the 'Pocket Handkerchief Tree'.

After the riot of bloom which fills the woodland garden during the spring and early summer the display continues with lilies and specimens of *Cercidiphyllum*, with hostas everywhere as ground cover. Outstanding in the autumn, particularly among the rhododendrons to the east of the Norwich Gates, are beds of hardy fuchsia, a recent addition, and wonderful hydrangeas. The woodland garden especially shows how the trees and shrubberies originally planted around the perimeters of the gardens to ensure the privacy of the house have been elevated to become areas of real beauty, rather than as they often were, masses of dense, rather gloomy foliage. Week after the week the gardens are a delight to either the ardent horticulturalist or to the casual visitor who is happy to wander among the glades, enjoying the natural repose of the setting.

Despite the changes, Sandringham House and the gardens retain their Edwardian flavour in the face of the ever-growing need for modernity and commercial success which faces the whole estate. The gardens are maintained in an exemplary manner by the present staff of fifteen gardeners. In the huge new range of aluminium glasshouses in the east gardens, quantities of pot-plants and cut flowers are produced in a system whose hyper-efficiency contrasts with the extravagant grandeur of the now sadly redundant teak Persimmon range. It is Sandringham's size which allows the shadows of the past to retain such an influential hold on the place. For King Edward VIII the family Christmases at Sandringham were always 'Dickens in a Cartier setting'. But in a sense Sandringham is no different from any country house supported by its own estate and surrounded by gardens upon which the family have had an influence and left marks of their characters.

BARNWELL MANOR

Northamptonshire

BARNWELL LIKE SO MANY rural manor-houses throughout England, has a history stretching back to medieval times. Its name was quaintly supposed to reflect the reported local custom of dipping bairns into wells, but a more plausible derivation is from the earlier Byrnewilla, reported *circa* 970 as 'the stream by the burial mound'. During the Middle Ages a great proportion of the land in England was held by powerful monasteries and abbeys of various religious orders, and from the beginning of the eleventh century Barnwell was owned by the Benedictine Ramsay Abbey in Huntingdonshire.

About 1170 Barnwell was let by the Abbey 'as an inheritance' to Reginald le Moine; his fourth direct descendant to hold Barnwell was Berengarius le Moine, builder of Barnwell Castle which today stands amongst the gardens to the north-west of the manor-house. Both the circumstances and the timing of the construction of Berengarius's castle are of some interest. It appears the castle was completed in or around 1266, in which case it was, as Sir Nikolas Pevsner described in the Northamptonshire volume of his series *The Buildings of England*: 'the first example in Britain of the most monumental type of castle architecture, the type with a more or less square plan and round corner towers'.

Berengarius's ambitions would seem to have been the establishment and expansion of local power, and it was only through the continuing connection with Ramsay Abbey that reference to any sort of gardens around the castle appeared. In 1264 the Abbey scribes drew up an inventory/valuation of the castle together with a list of freemen, coterels and borders. As was common practice in those days, the surname of a man often denoted his trade or profession. Among the list of twenty-three

Opposite : Looking past one of the bastions of the castle at the west end of the garden to the spire of Barnwell St Andrew church

coterels appeared the names of Robert Gardener and Widow Gardener, and further on in the inventory was mention of 'in the corner next the Chapel are 6250 sods of turf, value 1/8 per thousand', which were apparently to create a forelawn.

More specific references appear in a document of 1276, the year which saw the end of Berengarius's position of power at Barnwell. A Royal enquiry reported that Berengarius had built his castle without the necessary license, and as a result he was forced to convey it and three manors to William, Abbot of Ramsay – Barnwell's first brush with monarchy. Some compensation to Berengarius may have been the extraction of a handsome payment of £1666 18s 4d, and eight hogs heads of wine. The conveyance contains the passage: 'To have and to hold in pure, free and everlasting charity, with homage rents and services due, buildings, walls and ditches, in whatever manner raised or dug, meadows, pastures, paddocks, vineyard, orchard, gardens dug or undug, shrubs, pathways, woods ...'

It is easy to believe that the castle, now a partly-ruined survivor from the dark medieval past, is haunted. One chilling story relates how Berengarius le Moine walled-up his wife, alive, in a concealed room between the walls of the south-east bastion of the castle; and it is certain that a Marie le Moine, alleged wife of one of the le Moine lords, died in 1245, when the castle was likely to have been in the process of construction.

'From Leighton to Barnwell by exceeding fair corn ground. At Barnwell remain yet four strong towers of Berengarius le Moine's castle. Within the ruins is a meane house for a farmer.' Little seems to have changed since the beginning of Barnwell's decline in the mid-fourteenth century when John Leland visited Barnwell in 1539. Leland was the Surveyor-General to Henry VIII and was responsible for reporting on all abbey and church lands prior to the dissolution of the monasteries. Barnwell was granted to Edward Montagu, Henry's Chief Justice. Inhospitable and virtually uninhabitable, it was greatly improved by Montagu's son, Sir Edward Montagu, who came to be known as the 'Beautifier'. Sir Edward abandoned the castle altogether and to the east of its forecourt built a manor which forms the central three-gabled section of the present house. Around the new house Sir Edward laid out gardens in period style, the whole work being undertaken to celebrate the honour of knighthood conferred upon him by Elizabeth I in 1568. Camden, in 1586, recorded Sir Edward's improvements when he wrote, 'Neere adjoining Owndell stands Barnwell, a little castle which now of late Sir Edward Mont-acute (of the ancient family of the Mont-acutes as may be collected by his *Armes*) hath of late repaired and beautified with new buildings.' That Camden was in fact referring to the manor-house and not the castle is fairly certain from the fact that the arms he describes were placed above its main door on the west side. Also the new buildings were in very close proximity to the castle and would have been described as part of it; the distinction between manor and castle was not drawn until a later date.

By the seventeenth century Barnwell was established as a typical manorial world, controlling the neighbouring parish of Barnwell St Andrew. The castle, no longer inhabited, dominated the western aspect of the house. Sir Edward Montagu's son was created 1st Lord Montagu of Boughton (the Montagus' main seat since 1528), but spent much of his time at Barnwell, referring to it in his letters as, 'the place where I now live'. That he probably made improvements to the gardens and buildings is reflected in a letter he received from Sir Anthony Palmer; it ends: 'And so I leave you to enjoy and reflect upon your works at Barnwell.' Lord Montagu was to fall foul of the Parliamentarians during the Civil War for his fervent support of the Royalists, which included allowing the latter to store small-arms and muskets in the guardrooms of the castle gate-house. At an advanced age he was imprisoned by the Parliamentarians in Savoy House, where he died in 1644.

Lord Montagu's son William ensured the healthy maintenance of Barnwell and its gardens as his father and grandfather had done before him, but when Ralph, 3rd Lord Montagu and 1st Duke of Montagu, inherited the family estates in 1683 it took second place to his ambitious projects at Boughton. Ralph Montagu's years at the courts of Versailles and St Cloud as Charles II's Ambassador Extraordinary inspired the distinctly French north wing of Boughton House, and the extensive gardens there were laid out in the new French style pioneered by André le Nôtre. During these years Barnwell declined; the house was inhabited by an agent – William Stanley – and Ralph Montagu began the demolition of the castle, stripping off the facing stones of the inner curtain walls and knocking down a large section of the west curtain wall.

A print of Barnwell by the brothers S. and N. Buck which appeared in 1729 gives clear evidence of this partial demolition. It also shows, running parallel to and the whole length of the north curtain wall, an area of walled garden. The garden ran along the old dry moat which had been filled in, levelled and enclosed. It is possible that this garden had been laid out by 'The Beautifier' to serve his newly-built manor-house, or by his son, the 1st Lord Montagu.

Luckily the 2nd Duke did not continue Ralph's demolition work (which he complained about to William Stukeley in 1748 when the latter was visiting Barnwell), but the large gap in the west wall was not repaired for some time. Around the middle of the eighteenth century additions were made to the house which form the central part of the east front today, with its distinctive bow. By the end of the century Barnwell had passed through two generations of female heiresses to the Buccleuch family; Henry Douglas-Scott, 3rd Duke of Buccleuch and 5th Duke of Queensberry had married Elizabeth, grandaughter of the 2nd Duke of Montagu. It was probably around that time that the walls of the old garden along the north side of the castle were taken down and the rubble used for the raised terrace which now divides the castle from the kitchen garden. Little occurred during the nineteenth century to alter Barnwell's role as an appendage to the main Buccleuch seat at Boughton. The house was lived in by successive agents of the estate, who ensured the maintenance of the grounds, it returned to the family only once: the second son of the 4th Duke of Buccleuch, Lord Henry James Montagu-Douglas-Scott, who became 2nd Lord Montagu, lived briefly at Barnwell and died there in 1845.

But in 1890 the Earl of Dalkeith, who later became 7th Duke of Buccleuch, rented the property to Colonel and Lady Etheldreda Wickham on a twenty-one year lease. Sadly little survives in reference to the Wickham's tenure of Barnwell, for by all accounts the redoubtable Lady Ethel was a notable gardener. This may be seen in her work at Cottestock Hall, close to Barnwell, where she moved after leaving Barnwell in 1910. At Cottestock Lady Ethel designed the wonderful double, mixed and herbacious border; every year she spent hours with Mr Moore, her head gardener, poring over maps which she had made of the border, planning the next year's composition.

Lady Ethel, who died in 1961 at the age of ninety-eight, was the daughter of the 10th Marquess of Huntly, ('the Cock o' the North'); longevity would appear to be a strong-point of the family, for her father had been born in 1792. Thus 169 years spanned the two generations. It is extraordinary to think that she survived until the 'swinging sixties' while her father fought at the Battle of Waterloo, and her grandfather had danced with Marie Antoinette. Lady Ethel's brother, the 11th Marquis, who died aged eighty-nine, continued to astonish people well into his old age by insisting on walking from King's Cross station to the House of Lords, to avoid the expense of a cab fare. In 1910 the Wickhams' lease ended; in the same year Barnwell's links with Boughton were severed by the sudden sale of the manor and 3000 acres by the Earl of Dalkeith. It was rumoured that the sale was prompted by the Earl's nervous anticipation of the effects of Lloyd George's notorious 'People's' Budget of 1910, which threatened a Land Tax and the increase of direct taxation of the rich.

Barnwell was purchased by Horace Czarnikow, a wealthy Polish Jew, largely for the hunting with the Pytchley. During ten years at Barnwell Czarnikow made a number of alterations and additions to the house and was responsible for much of the form of the present gardens. Along the north side of the kitchen garden he built the range of teak greenhouses which today supply the house with a wealth of plants and cut flowers, and protect a number of healthy vines. Also, in 1913 the east front of the house was enormously enhanced by the addition of the broad balustraded terrace, whose flight of steps to the lawn and central sundial are aligned with the Georgian bow, giving unity to the varied architecture. He also planted the series of yew hedges which divide the lawn to the north-east of

Blossom overhanging a pair of beautiful wrought iron gates which open onto a path leading to the east terrace the house into sheltered paths and enclosures. The hedges continue the feeling of simple formality which the stone balustrade of the terrace lends to the east front. The regularity of their pattern, their low perspective and long rectangular shape contain none of the intricacy or bravado which so often characterizes topiary and which at Barnwell would disturb the placid atmosphere. It may not be too fanciful to imagine that the hedges consciously reflect the shape of the castle, which is visible between the north wing of the house and range of stables, the lengths of yew being broken at regular intervals by 'bastions' which are wider and higher than the yew 'walls'.

Thus Czarnikow's altertions determined the appearance of the gardens

to the east of the house. His wealth ensured that the house and grounds were immaculately maintained; it also appears to have afforded him a certain measure of eccentricity – in 1915 he had a stone house in the village removed and re-erected in the grounds of the manor for his butler. But despite his work at Barnwell Czarnikow did not make it his permanent home, selling it in 1920 to Major and Mrs McGrath. The McGraths also only kept Barnwell for ten years, selling the manor in 1930 to Major Colin Cooper.

Like Czarnikow, Cooper was a man of considerable wealth. He was also enormously active; he kept a pack of harriers at Barnwell, which he exercised each morning before leaving for London; built the hard tennis-court in the enclosed interior of the old castle, and put in the swimming-pool in the north-east part of the gardens. The swimming-pool was designed, in the style of the inter-war period, as much as a piece of garden architecture as a place of refreshment, and aspires, with its rich stone-work, twin changing-houses and tall enclosing hedges, to emulate Sir Philip Sassoon's famous Roman pools at his house in Kent, Port Lympne. During Cooper's time the number of gardeners totalled fifteen under Mr Mann, the head gardener – a very large labour force even considering the employment crisis resulting from the depression. Eight years after his purchase of the manor Major Cooper died on safari in Kenya. His ashes were scattered from an aeroplane over Barnwell woods, whose covers had given him so much pleasure during his short tenure.

The purchase of Barnwell in that same year, 1938, by Prince Henry, Duke of Gloucester, brought a renewal of ties with four hundred years of Montagu and Buccleuch history: his wife, Princess Alice, had formerly been Lady Alice Montagu Douglas Scott, daughter of the 7th Duke of Buccleuch, the same Earl of Dalkeith who had sold Barnwell to Czarnikow when Princess Alice was nine years old.

For the Gloucesters Barnwell rapidly became a world of private enjoyment and ambitions in the same way that, among others, Balmoral had for Queen Victoria and Prince Albert, and the Royal Lodge had for King George VI and Queen Elizabeth. Since their marriage three years earlier they had sought a country home. Barnwell, secluded, attractive, a manageable size and surrounded by farmland, provided both a refuge and an interest.

Alterations to the interior of the house went hand-in-hand with plans for the gardens, the farming and the upkeep of the estate. The Second World War took the Duke of Gloucester away from Barnwell – and often away from England – save for a few fleeting visits. Even during those busy, dangerous years Prince Henry's letters to his wife constantly made mention of what had unquestionably become his home: 'How I long to be home to see it when all the spring flowers are out.' When he was in England Barnwell was always his first priority, and whenever possible the Duke and Duchess improved the house and gardens, as well as the farm.

By 1947, when Queen Mary visited Barnwell, she was able to say that the Duke and Duchess had transformed their home in a manner she would not have thought possible before the war. During that year the Duke had levelled the piece of ground between the house and the road running below the garden's edge into a manageable slope, and had planted a spring and autumn shrubbery along the drive, where cherry blossom and the delicate silver of a weeping pear enliven the approach to the house.

Over the years the Duke and Duchess worked steadily on

The blend of pastel colours – here *Malus floribunda* with the stonework of the castle, was one of the Gloucesters' most effective additions at Barnwell

Contrasting features of spring blossom and the rugged stonework of the ancient castle. Just visible beyond the yew hedge which borders the kitchen garden is the delicate flush of *Malus floribunda*

Espalier apple trees smothered in white blossom in front of Czarnikow's extravagant teak houses

improvements and extensive new planting. The flatness of the perspective throughout the gardens and the subdued tone of the stonework of the house and castle cried out for the addition of colour to provide both warmth and character. The relationship between the house, castle and the very prominent spire of St Andrew's church – which appears in so many views across the gardens – meant that the gardens lacked some definite focal-point, and as a result the various areas required individuality. This the Duke and Duchess determined to provide.

The walls of the old castle lent themselves to adornment with clinging plants and borders. Two venerable pear trees, estimated to be over three hundred years old were already trained against the bastions; their age in no way impaired their display of blossom, and they were soon joined by the white and pink of aubretia and the pink and red of valerian. Along the south wall of the castle a deep bed of irises was added, which thrived in the alkaline soil. A mixed border of herbaceous plants and shrubs below the west wall faces a group of flowering cherries, whose blossom is accompanied by daffodils filling the grass around them.

The view out over pastures from the western end of the gardens features a collection of ornamental and flowering trees planted by the Duke and Duchess. One of these, a *Metasequoia glyptostroboides*, brings Lady Ethel Wickham into the story of Barnwell once again. In 1953 she gave the tree to Prince William of Gloucester and since then it has shown rapid growth. Another tree close to the *Metasequoia* is a fine *Catalpa*, in August covered with a mass of white flowers.

Where the long walled garden shown in the eighteenth-century print of Barnwell once stretched, the Duke and Duchess planted a long herbaceous border to the far western end of the gardens. Along the terrace thrown up when the old garden walls were demolished a yew hedge marks the boundary with the kitchen garden. Parallel to the hedge, and in contrast to its solidity and deep green is an avenue of *Malus floribunda*. In April and May their delicate pink blossoms blend in pastel harmony with the shades of yellow, grey, mauve and white in the border below. The display of blossom which is such a feature of the gardens at Barnwell is, surprisingly, at its most spectacular within the walled kitchen garden. Here the meticulously maintained plots of vegetables are surrounded by rows of espalier apple trees of numerous varieties. Seen from the raised vantage point of the terrace on the castle side during the weeks of spring the whole area seems awash with blossom.

Taking full advantage of the stonework settings open to them the Gloucesters chose a variety of climbing roses to be trained against the west and south facing walls of the stable block; also on the west side a *Carpentaria* produces delicate white flowers to accompany the roses. At the far end of the stables, facing the yew hedges laid out by Czarnikow, is a border dominated by another most attractive flowering shrub, a

Diplodinea. Czarnikow's balustraded terrace, too, on the east front of the house offered great scope. The space between the pavings of the terrace have been filled in with numerous alpines and in its centre is a simple sundial, typical of Barnwell's unpretentious character. More striking are the exuberant colours of the climbing roses, honeysuckle and clematis swathing the balustrade itself, and the strident peonies in the border along the front of the terrace. In contrast, the lawn stretching from the terrace only serves to underline Barnwell's general air of repose, and the spreading canopy of a sycamore is the only interruption in the clear vista to the rising parkland.

Perhaps the corner of Barnwell's gardens most cherished by the Duke and Duchess was the Silver Wedding Garden, a gift to them in 1960 from

The Silver Wedding Garden, a tribute to Prince Henry and Princess Alice

the staff of Barnwell. Secluded and intimate, the little garden is enclosed by a low yew hedge, its small beds laid out between paved paths and a central stone well-head. The bright yellow flowers of atrimollis offset the fine silver foliage of artemesia, while the emphasis on the miniature is maintained by a small shrub *Philadelphus*. The whole garden is shaded in the summer by the overhanging branches of a purple lilac.

The Duke's main interest at Barnwell had always been the farming, but he viewed the place as a whole much as his grandfather, King Edward VII, his father, King George V, and his brother, King George VI, had Sandringham. In a sense Barnwell provided the outlets – albeit punctuated by numerous and often prolonged absences – which members of the Royal Family have always sought and which have always been so welcome. Barnwell was the base for the Gloucesters family life. It was developed as a private place, essentially simple and rural. The life of a country squire appealed to the Duke and he was never happier than when helping with the harvest at Barnwell, hearing about the progress of his pedigree Guernsey herd, or watching the annual cricket match between the Barnwell and Sandringham estates. Thus the part Barnwell played in the locality came to reflect the characters of the family. Barnwell was never intended to be on a grand scale like Sandringham, but the similarity between the two properties lies in its progress as a country home. Gardens have always been Princess Alice's great love and she has tended those at Barnwell with great sensitivity. Today, aged eighty-one, Princess Alice is in the gardens as much as possible, weeding industriously or collecting flowers for the house beneath the wide brim of a straw hat, with an energy which makes her age hard to believe. Like the Queen Mother, Princess Alice has always believed that a garden demands personal activity to be enjoyed to the full, and has not been content to allow others to cope with the challenge of tidiness and maintenance while simply enjoying the fruits of their labours herself.

Since 1976 there had been at Barnwell a plant of which Princess Alice must be very proud, and which is a tribute to her activity in the world of horticulture. It is an unnamed rose seedling grown by Harkness New Roses Limited which will eventually be named in her honour. The seedling at Barnwell is the only one in cultivation outside the Harkness nurseries, the strain was raised by crossing the *Hulthemia* (*Rosa*) *persica* with the *Rosa rugosa* 'Harvest Home'. The *Hulthemia* is a native of Iran, South Russia and Afghanistan and is quite unusual in Britain. The new seedling not only has great rarity value but produces exquisitely small peach-pink flowers with a darker flush around the base of each petal.

Parts of Barnwell's gardens around the perimeters have become slightly overgrown in recent years because of reductions in the numbers of gardeners. But the patches of untidiness give the gardens an unselfconscious charm not apparent in gardens on a grander scale or more in the public eye. Winding shrub borders are a heady mix of lilacs,

The pastoral repose of Barnwell's surroundings

Overleaf: Looking across the Silver Wedding Garden and formal yew hedges to the east front of the house; beyond the ever-present church spire

viburnum and flowering cherries. Close to the swimming pool such a border leads down from the drive to a small opening of lawn where a single flowering cherry stands surrounded by healthy clusters of ariculas and primulas, which are an unexpected sight in a garden of light and quick-draining limestone soil.

Today Princess Alice's love of Barnwell and interest in the gardens are shared by the young Duke and Duchess of Gloucester for whom the house has become a family home accessible from London at week-ends, and it is easy to believe that their care and affection for its place will continue through future generations of the family. Although Barnwell has been Royal for only half a century, the family are very conscious of the generations of Montagu and Buccleuch ancestors who have held the manor before them. Barnwell is no trumpet-call of a Royal lifestyle but, in the manner of Frogmore or the Royal Lodge, a secure and welcome haven, which, throughout its long history, has not altered its fundamentally rural and provincial nature, so typical of the English shires.

ROYAL LODGE

Windsor, Berkshire

ON BEING ASKED when he first took a real interest in horticulture, King George VI gave the succinct reply, 'When I had a garden of my own.' That garden was at the Royal Lodge, in Windsor Great Park, which King George V offered the Duke and Duchess of York as their country home in 1931. In the next twenty years they were to show not only interest but a natural genius in its creation and landscaping. The work continued after King George VI's death, and today the Queen Mother continues to enjoy a garden which is a lasting tribute to a remarkable partnership.

It was over one hundred years before the Duke and Duchess moved into the Royal Lodge that it first enjoyed importance as a Royal home. Originally a red brick house in the style of Queen Anne, called the Lower Lodge, it was lived in by Thomas Sandby, the Deputy Ranger of the Great Park. The house was the appendage to the Great Lodge, which from 1746 was the home of George, Duke of Cumberland, Ranger of the Great Park, and by whose name the Great Lodge became to be known as Cumberland Lodge. During the latter years of the eighteenth century the occupiers of the Lower Lodge – Sandby was succeeded on his death in 1798 by Joseph Frost, Superintendent of the Farms – were closely involved in the development of the Great Park, and of its agriculture, a subject dear to King ('Farmer') George III.

The year 1811 saw the first in a series of developments which were to result in the radical transformation of the Lower Lodge. In that year, as a result of his father's worsening insanity (or porphyria, as we now know it to have been), George IV assumed the Regency and found himself in need of a home near to Windsor and London. The first choice was Cumberland Lodge, vacant at the time, but while the necessary reconditioning was

Opposite: One of the rides dating from the time of George IV. Great oaks shelter the more recent azaleas leading to the statue of Charity and the woodland garden

undertaken the Lower Lodge was to be prepared for the Regent's temporary residence. He never made the move to Cumberland Lodge, and during the rest of his life George IV spent increasingly more of his time at his lodge, immersing himself in plans for its architectural development and the wooded seclusion of its grounds.

Indeed from 1811 the house rapidly lost its identity as a lodge and became known, with derision by many members of the public, as 'the King's Cottage'. The Regency was to see the beginning of the age of the *cottage orné*, a fashion of which the emerging writer, Jane Austen, was very aware when she wrote her first novel *Sense and Sensibility*, published in 1811. In the book, Robert Ferrars remarks to Elinor Dashwood: 'You reside in Devonshire, I think, in a cottage near Dawlish. For my part I am excessively fond of a cottage; there is always so much comfort, so much elegance about them.' It is no coincidence that George IV was one of Jane Austen's most enthusiastic admirers, and in 1816 she dedicated *Emma* to him. The King's Cottage in Windsor Great Park was to become a supreme example of the *cottage orné*.

As with George IV's other architectural projects the development of the King's Cottage was financially a story of continuous escalation. John Nash, Architect to the Woods and Forests, was initially employed to make the necessary alterations to the Prince Regent's desires. In 1812 his original estimate, which included the cost of replacing the tiles of the roof with thatch – the first mark of a *cottage orné* – was £2750. By the year of Waterloo the figure had leapt to £35,243, exclusive of furniture (another £17,000). By Ascot Week 1815 the cottage was ready for the Regent's use; now the demotion of Cumberland Lodge was assured, for that was where the Regent's guests stayed and it continued to be so used for the rest of his life.

The frustrated Treasury must dearly have hoped that work on the cottage was complete. Little did they know that it would continue to be an object of the Regent's mania for building until his death. By 1821 more plans were afoot. A local paper of 2 April 1821 recorded the details, which included some changes to the garden: 'A covered walk, in a serpentine form, leading from the conservatory into the grounds, for the convenience of His Majesty and his visitors during wet weather, is intended to contain all the rare shrubs, flowers and creeping plants that can be collected.'

From 1823 the changes at the King's Cottage began to be related to George IV's plans for Windsor Castle. He had accepted the plans of an architect called Jeffry Wyatt for the restoration of the castle in preference to those of Nash, and largely as a result of this decided that Wyatt would be called upon to make much-needed alterations to Nash's original cottage – already in a state of disrepair caused by the thatch decaying. Because of the possibility of confusion with his uncle, James Wyatt, who had lately been Surveyor-General of the Works, and another uncle, Samuel Wyatt,

also a well-known architect, the King gave his consent to Jeffry Wyatt assuming the suffix '-ville.' 'Veal or mutton, call yourself what you like; it's all one to me,' was the King's reply. Public opinion on the King's extravagance and continual desire for change was shown in a satirical verse which appeared in a newspaper at the time:

> Let George, whose restlessness leaves nothing quiet,
> Change, if he must, the good old name of Wyatt,
> But let us hope that their united skill
> Will not make Windsor Castle 'Wyatt Ville'.

Part of the gardens of the Royal Lodge (then the Deputy Ranger's House) in the eighteenth century. A watercolour by Thomas Sandby

By the early 1820s the house was no longer called the King's Cottage but, for the first time, the Royal Lodge. It became obvious that the new alterations were designed to expand the cottage from what had always been a summer retreat to a main residence where the King would be able to spend many months of the year. It also rapidly became clear that a similar financial pattern was developing to that existing when the work on the cottage had been in the hands of Nash. By 1825 Wyatville's original estimate of £500 for the necessary repairs had risen to a figure of £15,000, as new ideas for changes and improvements constantly sprang to the King's mind. By then Wyatville had built a small chapel in one of the new plantations near the Lodge, for the King to worship in without having to go further afield to Cumberland Lodge or St George's Chapel.

It was not only to be nearby to supervise Wyatville's work at the castle that George IV began to spend more and more time at the Royal Lodge. He was happiest and most at ease when staying there. Not only did he love its secluded setting in a corner of the parkland forests of Windsor Great Park, he also took great delight in developing the grounds around the Lodge, mainly to enable him to drive through new plantations of trees and shrubs and along long wooded rides in his pony-chaise, at peace and away from the prying eyes of his subjects. For the King was increasingly sensitive of the discontent and hostility felt towards him by many of his people; it drove him increasingly to avoid contact with them in the refuge of the Royal Lodge. In the last years of his reign his desire for privacy became an obsession – at Carlton House he threatened with dismissal any maidservant caught watching him coming in and going out. In his book *Court Life Below Stairs*, J. F. Molley describes the King driving in the Great Park: 'When he went out in his pony-chaise if any persons were seen on the road the ponies' heads were turned sharply round and His Majesty drove in a contrary direction to escape even the casual glances of his subjects.' Thus the King determined to surround the Royal Lodge with woodland glades and paths not only to provide pleasant views and drives but also to hide it from the eyes of the world.

Visitors were rare at the Royal Lodge, and most of the time the King lived with the group which came to be known as the 'Cottage Coterie' and which included his mistress, Lady Conyngham, and her family. However, in the autumn of 1826 the King received one of his staunchest admirers, Sir Walter Scott, who afterwards wrote in his diary: 'Commanded down to pass a day at Windsor. This is very kind of His Majesty. Went down to Windsor, or rather the Lodge in the forest which, though ridiculed by connoisseurs, seems to be no bad specimen of a Royal retirement, and is delightfully situated. A kind of cottage, too large perhaps for the style, but yet so managed that in the walks you can see only part of it at once, and these well composed, and grouping with the immense trees.'

In 1827 Princess Lieven, who stayed regularly at the Royal Lodge and was one of the King's circle of intimate friends, recorded the events of one visit, giving another impression of the surroundings and an insight into their daily life: 'The site is pretty, fine, superb trees, very picturesque glimpses of landscape, a charming place. We led a lazy and agreeable life there, always in the King's society. Many promenades in the forest, on the lake, sometimes dinners under tents, always music in the evening, and in everything a habit of unspoiled magnificence, which left behind the sentiment of *une charmante béatitude*.'

The lake the Princess referred to was Virginia Water, one of the King's favourite places and the object of his constant attention. Much of his planning and planting in the grounds of the Royal Lodge was designed to give him the most attractive and enjoyable journeys possible to and from Virginia Water. The lake had originally been made by Thomas Sandby on

The informality of the woodland garden in spring: a bluebell glade amongst silver birch and beech

the orders of the Duke of Cumberland, who built himself a gazebo overlooking it called Belvedere Fort – later, in the wake of much alteration by Wyatville, this toy-fort was to become the retreat of King Edward VIII. By 1826 George IV had built himself a Fishing Temple by the lake, construction was in progress of a new bridge across the lake and there were plans for a new waterfall. In the same year the Ruins by the waterside were built from stones and columns which lay in the courtyard of the British Museum. And in 1828 a local paper described plans for another temple beside the lake: 'The King is going to erect a temple upon the verge of Virginia Water, from a pure and chaste design made by himself. The decorative part is given to Mr Chase. This temple is not only to constitute an attractive and beautiful ornament, but in case of need upon the Royal aquatic excursions on this fine lake, in the summer is to be converted to the *cortège* of the court.'

In 1829 Wyatville had completed his alterations at Windsor Castle and was able to begin work on what was to be the King's final addition to the Royal Lodge – a grand dining-room facing west across the sloping lawn and woodland glades beyond. It is a sad twist of fate that this – the only part of George IV's Lodge to survive intact – was not completed before his death. He died in Windsor Castle, frustrated by his inability to move to the Royal Lodge for the summer.

The death of George IV brought to an end the most eventful chapter in the Royal Lodge's history. There is no doubt that he had an extraordinary affection for the place because, unlike his other architectural projects at Windsor Castle, Buckingham Palace, Carlton House and the Pavilion at Brighton, it provided him with a home where he could be happy and at peace. His interest in it went beyond grandiose building plans; it was rather the creation of surroundings which were as pleasant for him as the house itself. And, of course, it had the added attraction of being a world of complete privacy, away from the venomous tongues of his critics. The value of George IV's development of the grounds of the Royal Lodge were to be realized a century later when, as Sir Owen Morshead says in *George IV and Royal Lodge*: 'A golden future was now at hand for the little remnant of George the Fourth's cottage, for in 1931 it was granted to the Duke of York (later King George VI) and his consort. In their devoted hands it has risen again into a house of grace and beauty, its bright gardens set amongst woodlands of the Regent's planting.'

But in 1830 all this was to come and prospects were very bleak for the Royal Lodge. The new King, William IV, had no need for the house, and within a year it was all demolished except Wyatville's splendid new dining-room and the conservatory. It is likely that Queen Adelaide had much to do with the demolition: she had little affection either for the late King or his mode of life, of which the Royal Lodge seemed to be the symbol. But even she was not immune to the attractions of the spot. In 1833 she celebrated her birthday there, and was later to add on a delightful room.

Opposite: Looking past one of the garden's enormous oaks and early daffodils to the pink-washed front of the house. The arched windows of Wyatville's dining-room stretch along the terrace from the old octagonal conservatory

What William IV had spared of the Royal Lodge was saved after his death by the Prince Consort. In 1840 he wrote to his father: 'I have saved the charming King's Cottage, with the greenhouse, which was to have been demolished as useless, by installing Anson there.' Before Anson (the Consort's secretary) was installed Queen Victoria had inspected the house and noted in her diary: 'It will do very well, though the house is very small. It is such a sweet spot and the garden is so nice.' Similarly when Anson left, three years later, the Queen 'went all over the house and into the garden, which was in great beauty, full of flowers. It is so pretty and peaceful.'

Queen Victoria maintained the Lodge for visits to tea when driving in the Great Park. It was looked after by a housekeeper, with a gardener and a man in the 120-foot long conservatory. In 1865 she unsuccessfully tried to persuade the Prince and Princess of Wales to take it on as a country home closer to London than Sandringham. From 1873 it was used as a grace-and-favour house for a series of members of the Royal Household until, in 1931, it became once more a Royal home whose potential for creating a garden was immediately appreciated by the young Duke and Duchess of York.

Once the necessary alterations had been made to the interior of the Royal Lodge the Duke and Duchess turned their attention to the gardens around their new home. They were faced with a formidable task because of the encroachment of undergrowth and weeds over the years past. Perhaps they were spurred on by friendly rivalry with the Duke's brother, the Prince of Wales, who a few years earlier had begun similar work of clearing the gardens around his new hideaway, Fort Belvedere. More important, the Duke's real talent as a landscape gardener soon became evident as areas were cleared to reveal vistas and paths, soon to be planted with an almost unrivalled collection of plants and shrubs. Neither the Duke nor his wife were content to plan and watch progress from a distance, but could be seen at every available opportunity – normally at week-ends – clearing rubbish, building bonfires and often leading parties of friends and household staff (willing or unwilling) in the work of reclamation.

The Yorks took great care to preserve and build on to many of the surviving features of the garden. The drawing-room, originally Wyatville's dining-room, and terrace look out on to a large lawn sloping away to the areas of woodland garden beyond, as they have done since the days of George IV. On the lawn stand two magnificent Cedars of Lebanon, and two enormous clumps of *Rhododendron luteum* which by their size, 12 feet high and 20 feet across, almost certainly date from the original garden of George IV. The work of clearance in the wilderness beyond the lawn steadily revealed the true quality of many of the standard trees, especially oaks – the Royal Lodge is blessed with some of the best in Windsor Great Park, in the freedom of their intended surroundings.

Around these trees the Duke built up the balanced and informal features of his woodland garden.

With a soil of sandy loam, locally known as Bagshot Sand, rich in humus, and gentle slopes and dells, the gardens were well-suited to the planting of shrubs which were always the Duke's speciality – in particular rhododendrons, of which he was to become a noted expert. His knowledge is wittily paraded in a letter written to the Countess of Stair in 'the language of rhododendrons':

Dear Lady Stair,

I must write and thank you both so very much for asking me to come to Lochinch, I did so enjoy my visit and you gave me such an *Agapetum* (delightful) time.

It was a great disappointment to me that my wife was unable to come too and she is miserable at having missed two *Formosum* (beautiful) days we had there. I am glad to tell you that she is much better, though I found her looking *Microleucrum* (small and white).

It was nice of you to say that I deputized well for her on Saturday but I feel that she could have done everything much better, as she has the *Agastum* (charming) way of *Charidotes* (giving joy). As we had arranged our visit for her, she *Pothinum* (much desired) to be there, and it was very sad for her to have missed it. However it is *Sperabile* (to be hoped for) *Timeteum* (to be honoured) with a future invitation.

As to my visit I am overjoyed *Eclecteum* (to be chosen out) and *Aberrans* (wandering) *Cyclium* (round) so many *Erastum* (lovely) and *Arizelum* (notable) gardens in so short a time, has left me *Charitostreptum* (gracefully bent) with a *Recurvum* (bent back), and somewhat *Lasiopodum* (woolly footed). I must say I am filled *Coeloneurum* (with impressed nerves) at all the *Agetum* (wondrous) and *Aperantum* (limitless) beauties of the gardens *Cyclium* (round) Lochinch.

But despite being *Asperulum* (slightly roughened) and having had time to examine my feet, *Denudatum* (naked) and *Detersile* (clean) I am glad to find that they are neither *Hypoglaucum* (blue beneath) *Hypolepidotum* (scaly) nor *Hypophaeum* (grey) but merely *Russatum* (reddened). This *Rufuscens* (becoming reddish) will have *Comisteum* (to be taken care of) otherwise they will not be *Eudoxom* (of good report) for *Clivicola* (living on hillsides) in August. As a diversion I much enjoyed our chase after the *Tephropeplum* (ashy grey colour) *Dumicola* (dwellers in thickets) which we were lucky enough to find *Telopeum* (conspicuous) *Lochmium* (from a coppice). Knowing you to be an *Ombrochares* (lover of rain) I hope you will soon get some to revive the Species of Rhododendron; which we are told by one Wallace: 'Of course it is over', and to make the snipe bogs *Paludosum* (marshy). It is too kind of you to have given me so many *Axium* (worthy) and *Eucallum* (beautiful) plants which will be *Eritium* (highly prized) by me and are most *Apodectum* (acceptable).

After this I feel I cannot write English any more. It was really too kind of you to have had me to stay and I did so enjoy every moment of it. Thanking you both again so very much.

Yours very sincerely
Albert[2]

One of the exquisite camellias in the Queen Mother's collection in the woodland garden

From the outset of their work in the gardens the Duke and Duchess of York received invaluable assistance from Eric (later Sir Eric) Savill, the Deputy Ranger of the Great Park. In the 1930s Eric Savill had begun the creation of what is one of the most remarkable pieces of landscape gardening in the country, the Savill and Valley Gardens. He shared the Duke of York's delight in blending trees and shrubs in a woodland garden; and he carefully supervised work at the Royal Lodge in the Yorks' absences, although he was the first to say that nothing was done that had not been planned or approved by them.

Over the years the Yorks built up a collection of excellent and often very rare specimens of plants and shrubs, in particular rhododendrons, azaleas and camellias. Many came from some of the great gardens in Western Scotland and Cornwall, normally as gifts from the owners, including the Bolithos at Trengwainton and the Williams at Caerhays Castle, both in Cornwall, the latter where the Duchess of York's original collection of camellias came from. A great number came from Lionel Rothschild's garden at Exbury near Southampton, which in its early days housed the world's first modest collection of specie rhododendrons. Many of the plants which went from there to the Royal Lodge had a fascinating provenance. From around the turn of the century Rothschild and a group of enthusiasts had started to grow rhododendrons from seed collected in the wild of the plants' natural habitat in Tibet, Burma, Nepal, China and India. Expeditions by men like Forrest, Ward and Wilson went out twice a year. First, they went in the spring and marked certain plants when in flower and identifiable. In the autumn they returned to collect the precious seed for replanting – often at Exbury. At the time of Rothschild's death the collection was really too big for Exbury and it was taken on by J. B. Stevenson at Tower Court, Ascot. On his death the Crown State Commissioners bought the collection; it now occupies twenty acres of the Valley Gardens, and is acknowledged to be the largest collection of rhododendron species in the world.

One legacy of the garden before the Yorks lived at the Royal Lodge is the great *Davidia involucrata*, undoubtedly one of the best specimens anywhere in the south of England. This tree, originally introduced into England from China in 1904 by Wilson is named after the Abbé David and is commonly known as the 'Pocket Handkerchief Tree'; the Royal Lodge tree stands among hybrid rhododendrons in the woodland garden, and in May the branches, which reach down to the ground, are a mass of white fluttering bracts.

As the gardens developed the Yorks' early efforts and ideas steadily began to bear fruit. Apart from his childhood plot of garden at Frogmore, the Royal Lodge was the Duke's first opportunity to indulge his own interest in and talent for gardening. His wife had been brought up at Glamis surrounded by the beautiful gardens of her mother, the Countess of Strathmore, who was one of the great gardeners of her day. At Glamis there were a series of gardens including an Old English garden, a Dutch garden and an Italian garden, all created by Lady Strathmore. There the Duchess of York, then Lady Elizabeth Bowes-Lyon, had had her own small garden from an early age. With a crimson rambler rose as its centrepiece she showed her love of flowers, in particular of roses. The origins of her knowledge and skill are shown in the remark she once made: 'My mother and grandmother were great gardeners and so I have always been interested.'

During the 1930s the Duke and Duchess of York gained invaluable help in planning parts of the Royal Lodge gardens from Geoffrey (later Sir Geoffrey) Jellicoe, the architect and landscape designer. The Duke of York had seen and admired Jellicoe's work at Ditchley Park in Oxfordshire, which prompted him to employ the architect to draw up plans for the Royal Lodge. Jellicoe was mainly concerned with the area closest to the house, and the establishment of a relationship between the pink-washed building with the lawns and woodland garden beyond. As a result the terrace and wall which drop to the gentler more expansive slope of the lawn below the main garden front give the house the appearance of an island surrounded by a sea of grass; but the dividing line is broken by

Protected by clipped beech hedges are the old-fashioned and species shrub roses of the Queen Mother's sunken garden. Beyond, the ageless forest trees and wide spaces of the Great Park

Looking south-east from Jellicoe's terrace across a corner of the rose garden. In the background, spreading acers, and to the right of the central conifer, the *Davidia involucrata* in flower

the flight of spiral steps leading down from the north end of the terrace, reinforcing the union of the house and its setting. Thus while the raised vantage point of the terrace gives the illusion of detachment it is at the same time drawn into the surroundings.

Below the terrace on the shorter, south side of the house, Jellicoe introduced the contrast of the secretive sunken garden, enclosed by beech hedges. Originally a mixed flower garden, it is now filled exclusively with roses, of which the Queen Mother is so fond. Here again the effective blending of the house and surroundings is visible, particularly in the mixed herbaceous and rose border stretching along one side of the sunken garden and softening the sharp outline of the beech hedge when seen from the main lawn. The border is also positioned to give a vista of colour from the french doors that open from the octagonal room on the corner of the house, originally the old conservatory.

From his work at the Royal Lodge Geoffrey Jellicoe gives a very telling insight into the achievements of the Duke and Duchess of York in their garden there. It was working with the Duke of York in the 1930s which was largely responsible for Jellicoe's developing interest in what he was later to call the psychology of landscape. At the Royal Lodge it was strikingly clear that the Duke and Duchess had definite and enthusiastic ideas about what they were striving to achieve in their garden, guided by three influences: the historical background to their home, its physical character and setting, and their personal desires and ambitions. It was the inspired fusion of these three motives which accounted for much of the Royal couple's love of the place and which held the key to their success.

As well as providing an outlet for the Yorks' gardening interests and ambitions, the Royal Lodge served another important purpose in giving them somewhere to relax undisturbed. Over one hundred years after the death of George IV it still retained the secluded tranquillity which he had sought so continuously. The calm early years of the Yorks' marriage, although busy with public duties, were soon shattered by personal trauma and national crisis – King Edward VIII's abdication, followed three years later by the Second World War. One of the occasions the Yorks met Mrs Simpson was at the Royal Lodge when King Edward VIII came with her to tea from Fort Belvedere, a few months before the abdication. The conversation was dominated by discussion of the gardens at the Royal Lodge and the Fort. Afterwards Mrs Simpson noted, 'that while the Duke was sold on the King's American station wagon, the Duchess was not sold on the King's other American interest'. After the throne had been thrust upon him, and during the war years, the solace of the Royal Lodge became even more precious to King George VI and his wife, and the chance of spending a week-end in the gardens was all they longed for.

In 1932 the gardens of the Royal Lodge gained a unique addition. To mark Princess Elizabeth's sixth birthday the people of Wales presented her with the Little House – *Y Bwthyn Bach*. A small replica of a thatched

Welsh cottage, it was the delight of Princess Elizabeth and Princess Margaret's childhood. Inside, each room was furnished; and in front there has always been a formal garden on the same miniature scale as the cottage, with flower-beds surrounded by tiny hedges and on either side wooden bowers hung with honeysuckle and climbing roses. Princess Elizabeth and Princess Margaret each had their own flower-beds and little areas of lawn to tend, as well as their own tools, and a small seat made by the Royal Wheelwrights on which to rest during working hours. When Queen Mary visited the Royal Lodge soon after the arrival of the cottage she was taken

Y Bwthyn Bach (The Little House), delight of Royal children for the last fifty years.

to look round it, but was sadly disappointed – for being tall and upright she could only go in as far as the tiny staircase. Recently The Queen's first grandchild, Peter Phillips, has revelled in the cottage's charms.

After the temporary neglect of the war years the gardens of the Royal Lodge enjoyed their real heyday in the 1950s and 1960s. Much of the design and planting of the previous years now reached maturity and the gardens showed the natural continuity which had always been the aim of the King and Queen Elizabeth. One of the benefits of informality was that new additions and alterations could always be made. In 1951 the Commissioners of the Crown Estates triumphed at the Festival Chelsea Flower Show, winning the Gold Medal with an exhibition by Eric Savill and his assistant T. H. Findlay, from the gardens in Windsor Great Park. In the woodland garden at the Royal Lodge the exhibit garden has been reproduced exactly, containing Kurume azaleas and dwarf hybrid rhododendrons and also an interesting innovation of the King's – bordering the beds with log branches to enhance the natural woodland setting. In 1951 another new addition to the woodland garden was the camellia garden, using many of the plants from Caerhays.

Today the gardens of the Royal Lodge clearly retain the individual charm and character which reveal both the ingenuity of their conception and the many years of devoted work the Royal couple gave to them. Other than reductions in the size of the woodland garden, because of the problems of maintaining such a large area, the creation of King George VI and his wife continue to give the Queen Mother's home a wonderful setting.

Along the west side of the house the terrace which replaced the old verandah is given a castellated effect by a row of small pinnacled box trees in square wooden tubs. Beyond the main lawn the paths into the woodland garden have an atmosphere of romantic mystery, often seeming to lead to invisible destinations between banks of rhododendrons and azaleas, or past single specimen plants between which open glades can be glimpsed beyond. In one area azaleas lead to a small dell where larger rhododendrons surround a *Metasequoia glyptostroboides*, a specimen of the rare deciduous-conifer tree thought to be extinct and visible only in fossil form until, in 1946, members of the Arnold Arboretum in the USA discovered it growing on the banks of the Yangste-Kiang river in China. Seed was successfully raised in America and the Royal Lodge specimen came from the Edinburgh Botanical Gardens – with Kew, one of the two places in Britain to receive specimens from the Arnold Arboretum. Nearby is perhaps the best rhododendron in the garden, *Rhododendron mollyanum*, around 24 feet high, with pink flowers and a very fine large-leafed foliage. Elsewhere a winding path suddenly reveals a small clearing with a single hybrid rhododendron 'Polar Bear' which, late in the season, in August, is a mass of beautifully scented white flowers, set against the blue background foliage of *Rhododendron cinnabarinum*.

The main avenue from the lawn into the woodland garden leads between banks of majestic rhododendrons to a focal point visible slightly uphill in the distance. Here a number of rides and paths meet at the feet of a statue of 'Charity', who looks back down the rhododendron avenue across the lawn to a glimpse of the house beyond. The statue is a copy of the original at St Paul's Walden Bury, the Bowes-Lyon family home in Hertfordshire. Behind the clearing around Charity is one of the older trees preserved in the reclamation of the gardens, a wonderful weeping beech, *Fagus sylvatica pendula*, whose branches sweep the ground.

The woodland garden is at its best in the spring and early summer when there is a rich variety of the rhododendrons, azaleas and camellias in flower, as well as many of the various specimen trees such as the *davidia*, a *paulownia imperialis* and a number of magnolias. Also at this time of year the glades and clearings are decked in some places by bluebells, and in others by daffodils of which the Queen Mother has a very special collection, in particular the miniature daffodils which fill one glade – Cherie, Karatoa, Chinese White and Pencaebar.

Closer to the house the gardens are more conventional, and show the Queen Mother's love of flowers in a mixture of their colours and scents. From the small formal beds of geraniums surrounded by neatly clipped lavender, on the terrace at the south end of the house, a small flight of steps leads down to the sunken garden, where the Queen Mother has replaced a mixed flower garden with a small old-fashioned rose garden. One of the roses found here is the unusual 'Sport of Elizabeth of Glamis', named after the Queen Mother.

The Queen Mother has also chosen roses for the east side of the house in what used to be her daughters' garden. Now there are three beds each filled with one rose, Iceberg, Pink Parfait and Evelyn. These beds surround the small minstrel statue in the centre of the lawn. Set back in one corner and flanked on one side by a bed of tall Queen Elizabeth roses is an aviary, reminiscent of the days when Princess Elizabeth used to have her own aviary of budgerigars.

The balance between the intimacy of the gardens around the Royal Lodge and the larger areas of open parkland and deep woodland beyond has always been one of its most lasting attractions. For George IV the Royal Lodge was set in a world of its own which he adapted to his tastes and designs. Over one hundred years later the Duke and Duchess of York were captivated in the same way. As a result the gardens around what was always their most private home are a very personal creation, something that is shown in a remark King George VI once made in conversation about the Royal Lodge garden: 'Now that really is my garden – I made it – go and see it.'

SAVILL GARDENS
Windsor, Berkshire

EVEN TODAY, in parts of Windsor Great Park, it is not hard to imagine the medieval kings hunting boar and stag amongst the huge forest oaks, some of which still survive from that time. This sense of natural antiquity was the backcloth to the creation in the 1930s of the Savill Gardens, in the south-east corner of the Great Park. They stand with the later Valley Gardens, as the outstanding example of gardens landscaped in Britain in the twentieth century, whose scale will surely never be rivalled. Equally important, the Savill Gardens reflect a harmony between Royal patronage and gardening interest comparable to the work of Charles II and William and Mary at Hampton Court. But while the gardens of the seventeenth-century monarchs were created for their personal pleasure, the Savill Gardens were made to be enjoyed by the general public.

Royal interest in the Great Park has been continuous since those distant hunting days and, particularly since the eighteenth century, has been responsible for frequent alterations and additions. Shortly before King George III handed over the profits from the Royal Estates to Parliament in return for the Civil List in 1760, the Duke of Cumberland had become the Ranger of the Great Park residing at the Great (later Cumberland) Lodge. This post has usually been held by the reigning monarch; today the Duke of Edinburgh does so. It was 'Butcher' Cumberland who, using his victorious soldiers from Culloden as labourers, ordered the digging of the lake that came to be known as Virginia Water which lies to the south of the Savill Gardens beyond Smith's Lawn. He also built the gazebo on its shores originally known as Belvedere Fort, which was later embellished by Wyatville and became the home of King Edward VIII.

Opposite: The austere trunks of the beech trees on the drier high ground above the upper and lower ponds, with shafts of light penetrating to a thick carpet of moss

The possibility of a garden within the Park, away from the Royal homes such as Windsor Castle, Frogmore and the Royal Lodge, was first conceived by Sir Eric Savill who became Deputy Surveyor of Windsor Parks and Woods in 1931, and Deputy Ranger in 1937. It was his inspiration and the enthusiastic approval of successive members of the Royal Family which were the motivating forces behind the creation of Savill Gardens. It is certain that neither of these factors would have succeeded without the other but together, and with help from many other people and sources, they achieved spectacular results.

Eric Savill left Magdalene College Cambridge, where his time had been broken by service in the First World War, and in 1920 joined his father's firm of Chartered Surveyors and Land Agents, Alfred Savill and Sons. His friendship at Magdalene with Owen Morshead, a direct contemporary, was to have significant bearing in the future. When Morshead (later Sir Owen) became the Librarian at Windsor Castle in 1926, Savill became a frequent week-end visitor and began his acquaintance with the various areas of the Great Park. Without this familiarity, which developed hand-in-hand with a growing interest in and affection for the park, it is doubtful whether he would have been in a position to accept the offer of the Commissioners of the Crown Lands to appoint him Deputy Surveyor in 1931. His decision to accept the post shows how large a part the Great Park had come to play in his life over the previous five years, for he left a secure partnership and took over the administrative and maintenance responsibilities for 15,000 acres, at a time when the growing Depression of the 1930s was beginning to affect agriculture as it did the rest of the economy.

Savill had not long held his new position when his ambitions to make a woodland garden somewhere in the inviting setting of the Great Park began to crystallize. He sensed a potential which, if developed, could enhance the Great Park and the public's appreciation of it with an area of exceptional beauty and horticultural interest and, at the same time, give him a life-long creative commitment. He was extremely fortunate that the members of the Royal Family who spent most time at Windsor – King George V, Queen Mary, the Prince of Wales and the Duke and Duchess of York – were sensitive to and quickly appreciative of his ideas: King George, as reigning monarch and Ranger of the Great Park, was directly interested in any project such as Savill envisaged, no doubt encouraged by Queen Mary and her interest in gardens; the Prince of Wales had begun clearing and making the garden around his new home at Fort Belvedere, as the Duke and Duchess of York were also beginning to do at the Royal Lodge; and it was their support which gave Savill the initial approval he was seeking.

It needed both inspiration and foresight to see a garden emerging from the thick undergrowth and huge Ponticum rhododendrons which covered much of the area he had chosen. There was to be no 'Cinderella' transformation; but if there was a daunting amount of work to be done, at least many of the necessary basics were encouragingly visible to the discerning eye. Lanning Roper has spelt out the factors which had influenced the search for a site, 'satisfactory soil, natural shelter from wind for tender plants, freedom from damage from late frost, adequate moisture and a high shade canopy for woodland plants. Water, either in streams or ponds, preferably in both, was highly desirable, for a woodland garden gains enormously in interest and in beauty from the motion and sound of a trickling stream, and lakes and ponds in a sylvan setting provide lovely reflections, a feeling of space, and those long vistas and broad compositions which are so restful and satisfying.'

In the small area of roughly twenty acres between the Bishop's Gate entrance to the Park and the Obelisk on the high ground above Virginia Water and the present Valley Gardens, there was an abundance of mature trees, particularly oak and beech, variety in the terrain and in places plentiful water which, with draining and containment, could be persuaded to form streams and ponds. Sir George Sitwell used to maintain that the choice of site is the most important prerequisite to the successful creation of a garden. Citing the examples of the gardens of the Italian Renaissance which he knew so well, Sir George stressed the vital relationship between the garden itself and the larger surrounding landscape in his essay *On the Making of Gardens*: 'It is only a part of the garden which lies within the boundary walls, and a great scheme planned for dull or commonplace surroundings is a faulty conception, as if one were to propose to build half a house or to paint half a picture ...; it is Nature which should call the tune, and the melody is to be found in the prospect of blue hill or shimmering lake, or mystery-haunted plain, in the aerial perspective of great trees beyond the boundary, in the green cliffs of leafy woodland which wall us in on either hand.'

Work began on the gardens in the winter of 1932. Initially it was largely destructive, taming the wild woodland jungle and clearing the rapacious undergrowth and bushes which choked and obscured so much of the natural form and charm of the site. Soon rabbit-proof fencing protected the area, within which the sites of bonfires between the standard trees which were to be retained marked the steady advance and opening up of clearings and rides. After the early felling the first of the major alterations to the landscape was begun: the area of the upper pond was cleared and the bog fed by a stream leading to the Obelisk pond dammed at the lower end.

By the spring of 1933 Eric Savill and his small team could survey their work with satisfaction: a newly-dug drainage ditch ran into the upper pond from the north-east part of the present gardens. Sir George Sitwell, like Lanning Roper, believed that water is the most magical and visually transcending feature of a garden, and the appearance of the upper pond in the Savill Gardens had immediate effect, bringing to life, with reflections

Overleaf: One of the Savill Gardens' magnificent vistas: looking towards the head of the upper pond, with azaleas and moisture-loving plants, and in the distance a wide glade shaded by tall beeches

in the gently stirring foreground, the lofty beeches on the far bank, their slender trunks dappled by light shifting through their full green canopies. Now could begin the choosing and siting of the new plants whose steady appearance resembled the development of the pattern of a jigsaw puzzle.

The new arrivals were carefully positioned so as to enjoy to the full the conditions to which they were particularly suited, and where they were displayed to the fullest visual advantage – dwarf rhododendrons beneath the shady boughs of old oaks, kingcups and primulas in the continually damp soil along the banks of the streams and ponds, and flowering cherries where their display of blossom highlighted a clearing or vista. The first kingcups arrived in the Savill Gardens in a manner which characterized much of the future acquisition of plants. It happened that Savill was bemoaning the lack of flowers in the gardens to Harry Wye, the Park Foreman, who quickly came up with the initial remedy. Disappearing on his bicycle laden with a basket of rabbits, he soon re-appeared triumphantly clasping dripping clumps of kingcups which a friend had been happy to exchange for the ingredients of a hot pie. Similarly the first of the numerous varieties of primulas which now thrive throughout the Savill Gardens appeared as the result of an innocent inquiry: having discovered that they were part of the spring bedding schemes in St James's Park, Savill asked Tom Hay, the Superintendent of the Royal Parks in London, what became of the plants when the time came for them to make way for the summer bedding varieties. On receiving the desired reply a lorry was quickly despatched to London, to return loaded with discarded primulas. The plants were all the Chinese *Primula denticulata*, and although they did not take to their new home quite as expected, one clump survives on the site of an old bonfire, where originally they thrived on the piles of wood ash.

The treatment of the first areas of the new gardens to be cleared set the style for all future developments. An immediate distinguishing factor of the Savill Gardens was that they were not laid out around or in the vicinity of a house which could act as a focal-point or dominating feature. In this sense, rather than growing into gardens as commonly envisaged, they took on an apparel more akin to an enchanted woodland. While many areas saw new plants, shrubs and trees brought to the gardens from outside, in other parts where wild woodland flowers – bluebells, anemones, etc – had appeared quite naturally, they were allowed to remain. The desire to preserve and, where possible, enhance the naturalness of the surroundings was paramount in the setting out of the paths and rides. Their courses were determined by the contours of the ground, and marked out by following the route which a man walking between two points instinctively took.

The work that was going on in the Savill Gardens in the early years was little known by anyone not directly involved, but it certainly did not escape the notice of the Royal Family, whose approval had been so

fundamental to the inception of the project. During the early months the team of gardeners had concentrated on the spring appearance of the gardens, the season so immediately sympathetic to a woodland setting, so that no longer was the threshold of summer heralded by a fresh advance of brambles and elders, but by clusters of crocuses and snowdrops around the protective trunks of the old oaks, as well as daffodils and the first early rhododendrons.

In the spring of 1934 King George V and Queen Mary announced their wish to visit the gardens. Frantic work before the Royal visit brought its reward. The King and Queen Mary were greatly impressed, not only with what they saw, which was an almost miraculous transformation, but also because they sensed it was just a beginning. Little was said as they wandered amongst the flowers and shrubs which their sanction had made possible, but on leaving Queen Mary's words, 'It's very nice, Mr Savill, but isn't it rather small?' gave him the encouragement he had been hoping for.

As knowledge of the activities in the Savill Gardens and the Royal interest in the work spread, presents of plants, in great quantities and variety, arrived from all over the country. They came from many of the private gardens with famous collections as widely spread as Cornwall and Scotland, as well as from some of the best known nurseries. It is doubtful whether any garden has benefited more from the generous influx of specimens as the Savill Gardens have and, coming from expert horticulturalists, the plants were of the finest quality and often rare or new breeds. People saw that the Savill Gardens had the exciting potential to contain unrivalled collections of many varieties, for instance rhododendrons, camellias, magnolias and primulas.

After 1936, when King George VI acceded to the throne and became Ranger of the Great Park, the continuing personal interest of the King and Queen Elizabeth greatly encouraged the general enthusiasm over the developing gardens. The appointment of Eric Savill as Deputy Ranger in 1937 by King George VI reflected the King's growing appreciation of the former's work in the Great Park, in particular in the new gardens. From very early days a relationship of mutual respect was established; and while Savill was always ready to give advice and to supply plants for the woodland garden being created next door at the Royal Lodge, and to supervise progress in the absence of the King and Queen Elizabeth, they took great delight, during week-end visits, in going round the Savill Gardens with him, discussing the relative progress of plants there and at the Royal Lodge, and giving their opinions of plans and ideas for the future. This invaluable assistance went far beyond official approval, giving as it did the encouragement of personal involvement.

The Second World War brought progress in the Savill Gardens to a virtual standstill, and even the efforts to keep the newly-opened and planted areas clear often failed. The work force was obviously drastically

Opposite:
Lysichitums, kingcups and primulas thrive in the shade and damp soil on the banks of one of the numerous small streams, calling to mind the original name of 'the Bog Gardens'

The upper and lower ponds: the presence of water bestows a feeling of depth and space to the surroundings. The still waters at the head of the lower pond reflect the slender branches of an alder and provide a perfect home for water-lilies and other aquatic plants which thrived during the enforced neglect of the war years

cut, and in his capacity as Deputy Ranger Savill had to turn his attention to the far more pressing need to improve the output of the agricultural areas of the Park. First of all this called for dealing with the deer who roamed throughout the Park and made any serious attempt to improve the farming impossible. As a result about two-thirds of the herd were culled and went towards the war-time food supply, while the rest were safely enclosed in a wooded area of about three hundred acres which had no agricultural value.

In the face of the crisis the Savill Gardens took on a sadly neglected appearance. Where irises and kingcups had once lined the edges of streams and ponds they now spread quite freely, as did water-lilies. Weeds re-appeared amongst the newly-planted areas and along the neat paths. And, uncontrolled again, rabbits found their way through the fencing, doing extensive damage to young trees and shrubs. The problems were further exacerbated by a series of dry summers, particularly that of 1946, when the relief of watering was not possible. Loss of plants through lack of water during these years made the provision of an efficient piped watering system throughout the gardens one of Mr Savill's priorities after the war.

Despite the problems it was not a case for complete despair. The unexpected growth put on by many of the trees and shrubs greatly enhanced the feeling of establishment in the gardens. No longer did the forest trees tower over diminuitive rhododendron bushes and frail magnolias, and a vista through the woodland areas revealed how the canopy was gradually blending on various levels. Other plants, which had become deformed through being allowed to grow too close to each other when the original intention had been to transplant some after a certain time, recovered their shape surprisingly well after being radically pruned back. In some areas it was discovered that many plants – azaleas and philadelphus for example – had spread extensively and produced numerous tiny seedlings.

Ironically the war damage provided one invaluable addition to the Savill Gardens, the long brick wall which now forms the northern boundary of the gardens. In the search for areas where rubble from the bombed areas of London could be dumped an enormous quantity of bricks came to Windsor and, using estate workmen to keep the cost as low as possible, the wall was built, with buttresses at regular intervals. Now the bays shelter numerous plants which depend upon the warmth and regular sunlight provided by the south facing aspect. Growing against the brickwork and in the raised beds below are an enormous variety of plants which originate from all over the world – miniature flowers which include many dwarf *Narcissus* species, dwarf shrubs such as the remarkable *Sequoia sempervirens*, 'nana pendula', herbaceous plants and climbers, one of the most brilliant of which is the *Tropaeolum polyphyllum* – a cascade of orange flowers.

One decisive step taken in the war years was the appointment in 1943 of T. H. Findlay as Garden Superintendent. A great deal of the gardens' wonderfully diverse nature and their success in the post-war years results from the formidable combination of Tom Findlay's mastery of plant cultivation with Eric Savill's talents. The end of the war also saw the return to the gardens of many of the old staff anxious to take up the restoration called for by the years of partial neglect. With an eye to progress in the existing gardens and possible expansion Savill impressed upon the Crown Estate Commissioners the need for greatly improved propagating facilities. These were soon provided and were invaluable in allowing the gardens to be largely self-sufficient in stocks of many plants.

What was emerging in the Savill Gardens, in a highly individual way, was the accumulation and fusion of the features and characteristics which had been steadily changing garden design and planting since the end of the nineteenth century, characterized by a desire to move away from the unexciting formality of Victorian flower parterres and to feature flowering and ornamental trees and shrubs, which formed the basis of the woodland gardens of which the Savill Gardens was becoming a unique example. Of particular interest were those native to the hills and forests of south-east and eastern Asia. Within the broad setting of the Savill Gardens there was scope for almost limitless variety of detail – detail of plant type and appearance, size and shape, position and effect, seasonal change and character, flower and foliage. It was not enough that a plant was rare or vulnerable, endowed with an exquisite blossom in spring or a striking bark in winter – whatever its individual qualities it had the equally important secondary role of fitting into the jig-saw whose picture was unfolding. In a sense the Savill Gardens can be seen as combining two aspects of gardens which in the past had normally been kept separate from one another – the creation of a landscape and the cultivation of plants of individual interest and distinction. Within a short while the paths, glades, banks and borders were presenting a kaleidoscope of both garden life and garden form. From 1947, because of their limited space the Savill Gardens expanded into the far larger area which lies between Smith's Lawn and Virginia Water, soon to be called the Valley Gardens. Plans for the development of the wooded slopes of the valley were on a far larger scale than for the Savill Gardens and would not have been feasible in the earlier years because of the sheer number of plants needed. These were to be mostly rhododendrons and azaleas, and for the larger specimens of rhododendron hybrids here was the perfect setting with relatively unlimited space. At the same time the Windsor Park Gardens saw work begin on what is now one of the most spectacular areas, the Kurume Punch Bowl – a huge, natural semi-circular amphitheatre which has been filled with thousands of plants of Japanese Kurume azaleas from a collection known as 'the Wilson Fifty' in honour of E. H. Wilson, who originally collected them from Japan. In early May when the kurumes are at their peak the swell of garish colour in the Punch Bowl is a brilliant, if slightly startling, sight.

All this activity outside the Savill Gardens did not mean that progress there was slowing down. Rather the opposite, with the various areas of the gardens gradually – and in some places rapidly – taking shape, with additions and refinements continually being made. In a sense it was the success of the original Savill Gardens which had spurred on the expansion of projects into the new areas. Already in 1951 it was clear that both the gardens were destined to become far more diverse and illustrious than their somewhat unfortunate name 'Bog Gardens' suggested; and that their emergence owed an overwhelming amount to Eric Savill. In a speech opening York Hall, the recreation centre built in the village in Windsor Great Park, King George VI announced that from then on the original Bog Gardens were to be called the Savill Gardens, in recognition of their creator's achievement.

Also outside the Savill Gardens and adjoining the Valley Gardens, was the area prepared in the early 1950s to receive what was perhaps the most horticulturally important addition to the Great Park – the collection of rhododendron species which J. B. Stevenson had accumulated and developed at his home Tower Court, near Ascot. Mr Stevenson had been building up the collection since 1918, largely with the aim of helping progress in the classification and grouping of the Rhododendron genus which seemed to be expanding unceasingly. On his death in 1950 his wife realized how impossible it would be for her to retain the collection, but, determined that it should stay intact, decided to sell it on the condition that the plants were not divided. At this point it was the intervention of King George VI which proved vital in bringing the collection to Windsor. Not only was the King acquainted with Mr Stevenson through their mutual gardening interest, but he also fully grasped the value of the collection and was determined that it should find a suitable home. To the King there seemed no better place for the collection than Windsor Great Park, where it would come under Eric Savill's care and supervision, and by the end of 1950 the purchase was successfully made. By the end of 1956 the enormous task of transplanting the collection had been completed with minimal losses, and Sir Eric (he was knighted in 1955) and his team could look with satisfaction on the two thousand plants and more including over four hundred and thirty different species, safely installed in their new home. The site afforded the plants far more space than had been available at Tower Court, and although rhododendrons were obviously predominant a variety of other trees and shrubs were blended with them. There is no doubt that Stevenson's collection was and is unique and, as Lanning Roper has observed, 'acknowledged by experts to be the largest and most comprehensive in the world'.

One of Sir Eric's main priorities was to develop and vary the seasonal cycle of changes to the full, so that throughout the year the gardens were full of numerous blends of colour and form. This was done partly by the use of individual specimens and also by building up areas of contrast

One of the paths winding through the older part of the gardens, where plantings impose a sense of order on the natural woodland

Opposite : Banks of
rhododendron colour in
the woodland garden
with, in the foreground, a
mass of *Tiariella cordifolia*

Above : The conical
flowers of *Hydrangea
paniculata* var. *grandiflora*

The delicate flowers of
Rhododendron yunnanense

within the gardens. Visitors to the Savill Gardens expecting them to be of an exclusively woodland nature would emerge from the primula glade or from a ride closely flanked by azaleas to be confronted with a wide vista across lawns broken by deep herbaceous and rose borders, bringing a note of traditional formality to the gardens, as well as a riot of mid-summer colour. The depth of the herbaceous borders allows for plants and shrubs of luxuriant size with, amongst the better-known characters, a number of unusual ones such as the *Poncirus trifoliata*, the 'Japanese Bitter Orange', whose orange blossom-like flowers appear in the spring. The combination of the herbaceous and the rose borders, filled in particular with old-fashioned roses and floribundae, give this part of the garden a very typically English appearance during the summer months. Their display is taken up in the autumn by the neighbouring border devoted exclusively to Michaelmas daisies – a mass of closely-grouped and vibrant shades.

Some of the Savill Gardens' rarest specimens are to be found in the raised beds below the brick wall, where the concentration of plants in a small area is a striking contrast to the more open woodland parts. In a sense the raised beds can be seen to contain in microcosm the emphasis on quality which is a hallmark of the Savill Gardens throughout; the wealth of plants is both intriguing and impressive. Among the most outstanding are the rare and tender *Paraquilegia grandiflora*, *Arcterica nana* and *Cassiope wardii*, the last two producing similar small white flowers in the spring.

The specialized nature of the raised beds focuses attention on the horticultural achievements which have been made in the Savill Gardens. In the main gardens these are combined with continual work on the composition of the landscape. As well as seasonal changes, alterations and additions subtly enlarge the variety of plant life presented on every side of the rides and glades, which is the key to the Savill Gardens. Many of the collections of various genuses which are spread through the gardens, or concentrated in areas to stress their individual interest, are renowned and in some cases virtually unrivalled. As well as the rhododendrons, both species and hybrids, whose numerous permutations of size and shape, flower and leaf are one of the most essential contributions to the gardens' appearance, there is the camellia collection, a gift from Ralph Peer of California. Included in the varieties is the rare Chinese *Camellia reticulata*, whose flowers blossom into seemingly limitless shades of pink in April and May. There are magnolias, a number of which are grouped in one part of the woodland garden; primulas, numerous varieties of which are found throughout the gardens, in borders, lining the banks of the streams and ponds or massed around a flowering tree to great effect, notably the purple of *Primula denticulata* beneath the early white blossom of a *Prunus* 'Mount Fuji'; and lilies, perhaps the most impressive of which are the towering and exotic *Cardiocrinum* (*Lilium*) *giganteum*.

Outstanding collections of various species are obviously remarkable in their own right, but it is the sympathetic positioning and blending together of the plants, shrubs and trees which remains the foremost expression of Sir Eric's genius. Visitors are able to take in fully the numerous vistas and points of interest because of the underlying naturalness which has always been a watchword of the gardens. At nearly all times of the year there are the surprises and unexpected appearances of unusual specimens among the commoner or more widespread genuses. In the early spring, when the gardens enjoy some of their most poignant and delicate views with crocuses and early daffodils appearing in the face of continuing winter, the splashes of colour provided by forsythia and dogwoods are enhanced by the more delicate yellow flowers of *Corylopsis* and the white flowers of amalanchiers or 'Snowy Mespilus'. Later on in spring one of the most beautiful sights are the white flowers of a *Halesia carolina*, the 'Snowdrop Tree', while early summer witnesses the clusters of pink flowers of the *Kalmia latifolia*, the 'Calico Bush', one of the best June-flowering shrubs for acid soils. Also in the late spring and early summer clumps of *Trilliums* and *Meconopsis* are in flower in the primula glade and other parts of the gardens. Among the best varieties of these are the white *Trillium grandiflorum* and deep blue *Meconopsis grandis*, and the former blends particularly well with drifts of Solomon's seal (*Polygonatum grandiflorum*). Erythroniums, of which Sir Eric was particularly fond, are similarly well represented in the gardens, and continually spread by naturally seeding themselves.

Such are the quantity and variety of plants, shrubs and trees in the Savill Gardens that it would be well-nigh impossible to cover them comprehensively. Seeing the gardens today it is scarcely creditable that less than fifty years ago they were a piece of overgrown scrub and woodland, and that in the intervening years such spectacular results could be achieved. 'The Windsor Gardens', said Sir Eric Savill himself, 'are not botanic gardens and should be thought of as private gardens accessible to the public.' And although the Savill Gardens are fundamentally different from other Royal Gardens, in that they were not created for a Royal home or residence, it is their Royal status which has been the decisive influence on their development.

FROGMORE

Windsor, Berkshire

FROGMORE WAS PART OF the Crown lands at Windsor during the reign of Henry VIII but it was not until two hundred and fifty years later when George III's wife Queen Charlotte acquired the property that the house and gardens took on their present appearance and became the most revered of all Royal retreats. There is a certain secluded magic at Frogmore, and a feminine quality in the chaste white house and sylvan grounds, endowed by the successive Royal ladies – Queen Charlotte, the Duchess of Kent (Queen Victoria's mother), Queen Victoria and Queen Mary – all of whom lived there or left memories of their lifetimes there. For Frogmore is a place of memories, peacefully living in the fond atmosphere of past happiness. Thus although the house now stands empty it is somehow never deserted, but continues in its reposed setting as a Royal sanctuary.

Its name originally derived from the abundance of frogs in the marshy moor to the south east of Windsor Castle. In *The Merry Wives of Windsor* two of Shakespeare's characters pass, 'through the fields ... through Frogmore', where they find 'Mistress Anne at a farmhouse a-feasting'. The site was referred to only because the old road from Windsor to Old Windsor passed by it, and it remained of little interest until the reign of William and Mary; the tenant, William Aldworth, decided to replace the old house, which had fallen into a state of decay, with a new one built of brick and in front of the house he laid out small formal gardens in matching period style. Soon afterwards Frogmore received its first inhabitant with Royal connections – George FitzRoy, Duke of Northumberland, the youngest of Charles II's bastards by Barbara, Duchess of Cleveland. The Duke's second wife bought the lease and lived

Opposite : The picturesque effect of Wyatt's Gothic ruin overgrown by wisteria

to the age of a hundred and five, dying at Frogmore in 1738.

For a short time in the middle of the eighteenth century Frogmore was the prison of the notorious French soldier Marshal Bellisle, who had been captured while on a mission from Louis XV to the King of Prussia. Horace Walpole described him as, 'England's most determined enemy'; after being imprisoned in the Round Tower at Windsor Castle (he was the last prisoner of the State to be held there), he was moved to Frogmore, where he paid a rent of £200 per annum, because of the expense of keeping him at Windsor – estimated at over £100 per day. Bellisle was released in an exchange of prisoners after the battle of Fontenoy. Upon subsequent sale Great Frogmore, as the house had come to be known, to distinguish it from the adjacent Frogmore Farm, became the property of Sir Edward Walpole, brother of Horace and son of the Prime Minister. He brought to the house his romantic but somewhat scandalous tale; he lived there with Dorothy Clements, a girl of unsurpassed beauty, who had been a poverty-stricken seamstress, and whose lowly birth prevented Sir Edward from marrying her. However, Dorothy's beauty was perpetuated in their daughters who became renowned in London society as 'the Three Graces', and inspired some of Reynolds' and Gainsborough's most captivating portraits. One of these three girls born with no worldly status was named Maria and described by her uncle, Horace Walpole, as, 'Beauty itself'. She married the Earl of Waldegrave but was widowed while still very young, with three daughters of her own. In her book, *Round and About Windsor*, Olwen Hedley describes how, during her widowhood, the Eton boys would crowd into St George's Chapel in order to see 'Lady Waldegrave at Castle prayers'. Her widowhood did not last very long, and her second marriage brought the Countess to an even higher social pinnacle, for she married William, Duke of Gloucester, George III's brother. Their son, Prince William, Duke of Gloucester married his cousin, Princess Mary. At the end of her Cinderella-like life the Duchess was buried in St George's Chapel with the ceremony due her as a Princess and it must have been hard then to recollect her unpropitious origins.

Sir Edward's Royal grandchildren most probably knew Frogmore well but he had sold the house in 1766. Twenty-four years later Queen Charlotte acquired the home near Windsor Castle she had been seeking for some time when she bought the lease of Little Frogmore (formerly Frogmore Farm), and on 4 May she wrote to Lord Harcourt, her Master of Horse: 'I have been so fortunate as to obtain from Mrs Darell the Garden and House at Frogmore.' After the Royal Family had spent Princess Amelia's seventh birthday at the cottage later in the year it was renamed Amelia Lodge. As soon as she took over the little house Queen Charlotte turned her attention to the garden, busying herself with building a greenhouse and filling the old kitchen garden with flowers.

Queen Charlotte had already shown her great interest in botany by her encouragement of the now world-famous botanical gardens at Kew. In

1773 the *Strelitzia reginae* was introduced from South Africa and named in the Queen's honour, and in 1784 Lord Bute, an expert botanist, asked, and was granted permission, to dedicate to the Queen the nine volumes of his illustrated *Botanical Tables*, which were the fruit of many years' work. Frogmore answered Queen Charlotte's desire for a retreat of her own, where she could be close to the King when he was at Windsor Castle and pursue her resolve to surround the house with new gardens, with the assistance of Charlotte, Princess Royal, who shared her enthusiasm. Another motive for taking on the little house was that Queen Charlotte needed somewhere to house the Reverend John Lightfoot's famous herbarium, which the King had bought for £100 on Lightfoot's death in 1788 as a gift for her.

For help with her botany, and during the early days of planning the garden at Little Frogmore, Queen Charlotte often sought advice from William Aiton, who looked after the botanical gardens at Kew. But from the spring of 1791 she gained the full-time assistance of another gardening enthusiast, the Reverend Christopher Alderson, who came to Frogmore from being the rector of Eckington, near Chesterfield in Derbyshire. Alderson had previously been curate to William Mason, who wrote lengthy books of poetry on the ideals of landscape gardening. Queen Charlotte described Alderson as 'a man of great natural taste but not of the World', and hoped, in the garden at Frogmore, that he would be able 'to render this unpritty thing pritty'.[3] The rector obviously began to make good progress for Queen Charlotte's letters not only reveal her enjoyment of her private world at Frogmore but also show how it was able to reassure her outlook on life, giving it a note of simplicity. Early in 1791 the Queen wrote from Frogmore to her son Prince Augustus, 'I am of the opinion that the best thing is to enjoy what I have and not to make myself uneasy about things in which no human power can direct. The real wants in life are few; sufficient for myself, and if possible a little more for the relief of my neighbour, is perfect happiness to me.'[4]

Life at Amelia Lodge came to an end in 1792, not for any disagreeable reasons but, on the contrary, because Queen Charlotte succeeded in buying from the Hon. Mrs Ann Egerton the lease of great Frogmore, whose far more extensive grounds lay adjacent to those of Amelia Lodge. The latter, now rendered sadly obsolete, was pulled down shortly after Queen Charlotte moved to Great Frogmore, and its gardens taken in with those of the larger house. Queen Charlotte's move to Great Frogmore heralded the changes to house and grounds which gave the place its present appearance; and for the rest of her life Frogmore became her favourite home, in preference to both Kew and the Queen's Lodge below the south front of Windsor Castle.

James Wyatt was commissioned by Queen Charlotte to make the desired alterations to the house, and it is to his hand that we owe the supremely graceful cream mansion which today looks on to the lawns and

Overleaf: Price's lake, bordered by luxuriant trees, reflecting the graceful façade of Wyatt's house

lake stretching away from its south façade. It is interesting that Wyatt's first plans for the new house were for a Gothic cottage, which Queen Charlotte rejected – although Wyatt's Gothic ambitions did come to fruition later at Frogmore in a different form. In the event Wyatt succeeded in enhancing the Dutch-inspired brick house at Frogmore into a rare example of Georgian elegance. One feature Queen Charlotte hankered after was a colonnade which, as she wistfully remarked, 'will make a Sweet retirement in the summer all Dressed out with flowers'.[5] Her wishes were answered in a most harmonious manner for thus prompted, Wyatt planned the garden or south front exactly as it is today, with a low central colonnade running the width of the old house between two new wings with bow fronts. The final rendering of the house in stucco completed the effect; it is interesting to note the similarity between Wyatt's style at Frogmore and another house he was building nearby, Stoke Park – also cream-coloured with a colonnade and bows.

The major task at Frogmore was to convert the flat, unexciting area of the grounds to the south-west of the house into gardens of interest and character. As well as benefitting from the assistance of Alderson Queen Charlotte turned to her Vice-Chamberlain, Major William Price, to design the new grounds and work began in 1793. When completed Price's creation was an impressive achievement. The narrow stream, which ran through the gardens with marshy ground on either side, was dug out to make the long, serpentine lake, and the earth from the excavation was used to form the island, banks and varying mounds which were the foundations of the emerging irregular landscape. The gardens developed with lawns and flower parterres, paths winding through thickets or past carefully positioned trees, and over the bridges which crossed the various stretches of the lake. Some of the garden features so popular at that time were also to be found there, including a grotto, a Grecian temple and a Gothic ruin.

Major Price's brother was Sir Uvedale Price, well-known for his *Essays on the Picturesque*. The essays were partly provoked by what Sir Uvedale considered to be the ruination of various landscapes being perpetrated by 'Capability' Brown and his followers up and down the country. Throughout the essays Brown reappeared constantly as the *bête-noir* and his work was subjected to numerous savage condemnations. In one instance Sir Uvedale recounted a story with which he no doubt agreed whole-heartedly. A certain gentleman meets 'Capability' Brown who is ruminating upon the extensive further alterations to the landscape he would like to make before he dies. The gentleman remarks to 'Capability' that he would certainly like to die before 'Capability' does; and on being asked for what reason replies, 'Because I should like to see heaven before you have improved it.'

In contrast to what he saw as the unnaturalness of 'Capability' Brown's landscape designs Sir Uvedale advocated the need to strive for

One of the pair of vases by Joseph Harris of Bath which stand sentinel in front of the bay wings of Frogmore. The tall windows of Queen Charlotte's treasured colonnade which stretches across the front of the house are visible

the 'Picturesque', discussing the subject from every conceivable angle. And although it is not always easy to extract clarity from the often tortuously long-winded writing, it is clear that Sir Uvedale strongly influenced the evolution of the landscape at Frogmore. The search for naturalness which Sir Uvedale considered 'Capability', with his clumps and belts of trees and sweeping lawns, had failed to achieve, led to the studied irregularity of pattern at Frogmore that was reckoned essential to the idea of the Picturesque. The contrast between Wyatt's Grecian temple and Gothic ruins highlights a section of Sir Uvedale's essays where he discussed the relationship between the Beautiful and the Picturesque. He proposed that as well as being partially inseparable, because variation is an essential theme of the Picturesque, their juxtapositioning was often successful. The justification for each building can be seen in two of his passages: 'A temple or palace of Grecian architecture in its perfect state, and with its surface and colour smooth and even, either in painting or reality is beautiful'; 'Gothic architecture is generally considered as more picturesque, though less beautiful than Grecian, and upon the same principle that a ruin is more so than a new edifice.'

The essays often discussed the writing of William Mason – the clergyman to whom Alderson had recently been curate – in terms of strong approval, and Wyatt's Gothic ruins seem to be in clear sympathy with one extract from Mason's poetry:

> 'Fronting this lake there rose a solemn grot,
> O'er which an ancient vine luxuriant flung
> Its purple clusters ...'

Tumbling from the stonework of the 'old' walls in the manner of Mason's vine are the tresses of a wisteria.

The achievement of the Picturesque was part of the rural world Queen Charlotte was trying to create at Frogmore; a '*Paradis Terrestre*' similar to Marie Antoinette's Petit Trianon at Versailles, to which it has often been compared. As well as the temples (there was also a Temple of Solitude) and Gothic ruins, Frogmore had a number of features designed to represent a world of bucolic simplicity: a thatched barn for dances, a thatched Hermitage designed by Princess Elizabeth (Queen Charlotte's daughter), and a corn-mill. Emphasizing the note of self-sufficient productivity was the printing-press inside the house. Among these carefully nurtured surroundings Queen Charlotte's days at Frogmore took on a sheltered pattern of restfulness and became her increasingly sought-after release from the pressures and problems of court life. If the weather permitted the Queen would breakfast in the Gothic ruins beside the lake, where the King sometimes joined her. Often she spent much of the day in the Hermitage or one of the little temples, working at her botany, reading, drawing or drying plants. She was continually collecting plants–many from Kew and some from sources overseas – and would walk or ride her donkey through the grounds studying their progress.

During her years at Frogmore Queen Charlotte held a series of *fêtes champêtres* in honour of certain Royal occasions. The first, which was postponed on the death of Queen Marie Antoinette, took place in 1793 to celebrate the anniversary of the accession of George III. For these occasions the setting of Frogmore must have taken on the appearance of an early-Stuart masque, with garlands of flowers adorning the colonnade of the house and the temples, and dancing, acrobats and extracts from plays.

Perhaps the most spectacular *fête* was that of 1809, to celebrate the King's Golden Jubilee. Although George III himself was unable to attend because of his blindness, the attendance at this *fête*, as at the others, typified relations between monarchy and people during George III's reign, for it was not limited to the court or aristocratic society but included those from all walks of life who lived in and around Windsor. During that evening Frogmore was clothed in fantasy; at the climax of the celebrations – as the

Reading Mercury described – there appeared, 'on a sudden, and as it were by magic, on the beautiful piece of water opposite the garden front of the house, two triumphal cars, drawn by two sea-horses each, one occupied by Neptune, and preceded by the other with a band of music'. As the boats sailed around the lake, Wyatt's Grecian temple on the island was lit with a transparency which the *Reading Mercury* (again) described as, 'the Eye of Providence, fixed as it were, upon a beautiful portrait of His Majesty, surmounted by stars of lamps'. Because of the King's illness his life became one of total seclusion and that was to be the last of the *fêtes* at Frogmore. But they had allowed the public an insight into Queen Charlotte's haven. With a myriad of lights flickering off the lake to reveal the pillar of a temple, the arch of a window in the Gothic ruin or the tall outlines of trees, and in the background the seemingly luminous cream house occasionally brilliantly bathed in light by a display of fireworks, Price's idyllic landscape showed itself to be the perfect stage for these nocturnal festivities.

As Queen Charlotte's life moved into old age she became steadily less inclined to leave Windsor, and in particular Frogmore. The house and grounds formed a world of her own, and in the years to come were to retain the lingering influence of her character. They show how styles had developed in the late-Georgian period, but more particularly they clearly provided something which had been lacking for Queen Charlotte, and reveal not only her tastes but a strong purpose in their creation.

An Act of Parliament which had been passed during Queen Charlotte's lifetime, granting Frogmore and the grounds to herself and her daughters, enabled her to bequeath it in 1818 to Princess Augusta, the eldest of the two unmarried daughters. Princess Augusta's devotion to her parents led her to remain in her apartments in Augusta Tower in the south front of the castle until the death of King George III in 1820; and for the same reason she determined that her mother's adored world of Frogmore would remain as little changed as possible. She was unable to prevent the sale of many of Queen Charlotte's possessions and the contents of the house, including jewels, furniture, porcelain, drawings and the Queen's wonderful library, but until her death Princess Augusta carefully preserved the memories of her mother and the evidence of her work which filled the grounds of Frogmore.

When Princess Augusta died in 1840 Frogmore passed to the Duchess of Kent, Queen Victoria's mother. During the Duchess's tenure Frogmore gradually began to show signs of the influence of Queen Victoria and Prince Albert, for whom the grounds became a favourite retreat, far more accessible than either Osborne or, later, Balmoral. Prince Albert built his model dairy in the Home Park close to the house. As well as admiring Price's steadily maturing scenery it is likely he added the mark of his affection for the place by planting some of the surviving standard trees, particularly conifers, which appear to date from that period – such as the tall

columnar 'Incense Cedar' (*Calocedrus decurrens*) which stands on the lawn in front of the house towards the island, and the 'Bhutan Pine' (*Pinus excelsa*) at the far end of the lake from the house, both of which were specimens introduced into Europe during the first half of the nineteenth century.

In March 1861 the Duchess of Kent died. She was buried in

A stretch of the serpentine lake; the stone bridge crosses to the seclusion of the island

accordance with her wishes in the mausoleum which Prince Albert had ordered to be built in the grounds of her home and which was virtually complete by the time of her death. The desire for a mausoleum originated with the Duchess's family of Saxe-Coburg, also Prince Albert's family. Prince Leopold of Saxe-Coburg had erected a mausoleum in memory of his wife, Princess Charlotte, the daughter of King George IV, at her home, Claremont; and shortly afterwards the Duchess's brother, Prince Ernest who was Prince Albert's father, was buried in a mausoleum which his family built in Coburg. Prince Albert commissioned Professor Ludwig Grüner to design the Duchess of Kent's mausoleum, and the architect was

A. J. Humbert, who was later to rebuild Sandringham House. The small building replaced Wyatt's Grecian temple on the large mound in the lake, in front of the house, and its simple circular shape, surmounted by a copper dome and enclosed by pillars, blended with the trees around it.

Far more momentous for Frogmore was the death in December 1861 of the Prince Consort. As early as 1843, though still in their early twenties and married only three years previously, Queen Victoria and Prince Albert saw Princess Charlotte's mausoleum at Claremont and they decided to break with the centuries-old Royal English tradition and be buried together in a mausoleum. Eighteen years later, shattered by the death of her husband, Queen Victoria could only draw hope from the thought of joining him in the future, and immediately began planning the place where one day they would be reunited and lie together. The Queen's choice of the south-west corner of Frogmore's gardens as the site for their mausoleum cast a sanctified spell over the place which she perpetuated during her widowhood and which it has retained ever since. Her choice was prompted by the Prince Consort's affection for Frogmore and the many happy hours they had spent there together; but more important for the Queen was the strength she drew from the proximity of Frogmore to Windsor, where she spent so much of her time in the subsequent years of her reign, and her ability to visit the tomb easily and regularly.

In continuity with what would have been the Prince Consort's wishes, about which on occasions the Queen was to become quite obsessive, the mausoleum was designed and built by Grüner and Humbert, the former

Opposite: One of the gnarled holm oaks in whose shade Queen Victoria's tent was erected, where she sat and worked

Queen Victoria working in the gardens of Frogmore, attended by one of her Indian servants

also designing the interior. Monumental but simple, the building was styled in the form prevalent in Italy in the thirteenth century, a square cross, with a central octagon, open to a lofty dome, surrounded by four small chapels. In the centre of the octagon was raised the huge tomb designed by Baron Carlo Marochetti. Initially it was surmounted by a marble effigy of the Prince Consort; the Queen's effigy was carved at the same time, and eventually when laid beside her husband's it preserved her image not as the old Queen but as the young widow.

Consecrated by the presence of the mausoleum and her beloved husband, the grounds of Frogmore took on a spiritual ambience and became a shrine for Queen Victoria during the rest of her lifetime. Over the years the picturesque mounds and banks of the lake became steadily overgrown with dense yew and laurel, forsythia and rhododendron, shrouding her in the privacy and seclusion she sought there, drawing strength from the enclosed solitude in close proximity to her husband.

The thick groves of yew trees and laurel, which in places threatened completely to obscure the carelessly winding paths along which Queen Charlotte and her daughters had wandered in the days when Frogmore was their solace, may have seemed to some almost to submerge its arcadian charm with gloom. But for Queen Victoria they ensured her undisturbed enjoyment of the grounds which she could reach in minutes from Windsor Castle. After the marriage of the Prince of Wales and Princess Alexandra in St George's Chapel in 1863, which she attended concealed in Catherine of Aragon's high closet, she lunched alone away from the celebrations and in the afternoon drove to Frogmore to pray in the mausoleum. Later on in her reign she built the small tea-house in her favourite corner of the gardens, to the south-east of the house. Driving in her pony-cart from Windsor she would go there to work at her papers in the same way as she did in the old gardener's cottage which the Prince Consort had built in the gardens of Balmoral. The typically Victorian tea-house, with its precociously tall chimneys, blended perfectly into the picturesque nature of Frogmore, and its cottage-style architecture reflected the Queen's awareness of the rural character Queen Charlotte and Major Price had given to the place. As often as not the Queen worked outside, under her tent, which was put up between the tea-house and the two huge gnarled holm or evergreen oak trees nearby. On those occasions the Queen was attended by one of her Indian servants whose memory is perpetuated in India Island at the bottom end of the lake, just outside the grounds. This was designated by Queen Victoria as the Indians' cemetery – their religion demanded burial in ground surrounded by water – although the purpose was never fulfilled.

Queen Victoria's role as Empress of India is marked with an Indian Kiosk from the Kaiserbagh at Lucknow, standing on the far side of the gardens from the tea-house beyond the Gothic ruins. Its exquisite oriental symmetry and perfect shape make an intriguing contrast with

The Duchess of Kent's Mausoleum, its architecture reminiscent of Wyatt's earlier Grecian temple

the preconceived decay of the ruins, and it is now offset by the rich green shades of a cedar and a wellingtonia. Lord Canning, who became India's first Viceroy at the end of the Mutiny, selected the kiosk for Queen Victoria from Lucknow after the capture of the city in 1858.

Thus Queen Victoria left her mark at Frogmore. But far more evocative of her influence was the curtain of shrubberies which concealed from the outside all but the tops of its trees and the green copper roof of the mausoleum where, after waiting for forty years, she was laid to rest beside her husband. During those intervening years Queen Victoria continued her pilgrimages, not only to the mausoleum but to work or rest in the shade of the trees she particularly loved and, after her death, the grounds of Frogmore gradually took on a hallowed quality. Thereafter successive generations of the Royal Family have been buried in the mausoleum's small cemetery under the spreading branches of one of the garden's beautiful plane trees.

In 1902 King Edward VII offered Frogmore to the Prince of Wales and Princess May (later King George V and Queen Mary). For the King, and for the Prince and Princess of Wales, Frogmore held a special, poignant importance, not only through memories of Queen Victoria, but also because in 1864 Albert Victor, Duke of Clarence and Avondale, had been born in the house – to his grandmother's delight. 'Eddy', the Duke of Clarence, an erratic young man who was engaged to Princess May, died tragically young from influenza and pneumonia in 1892; thus his younger brother, Prince George, became the heir-presumptive.

Frogmore became the official residence of the Prince and Princess of Wales during Ascot Week every year. Far more importantly, it offered – as it had always done in the past, to Queen Charlotte and to Queen Victoria – a haven, a refuge. The Princess was captivated by the grounds and as often as possible would come with her children to spend summer afternoons there. Soon after they acquired the house she wrote to her husband, 'It is too divine here and everything is looking lovely, the house charming and fresh and the garden and grounds a dream.' During one of her visits in 1905 Princess May made what was probably her first addition to the gardens. Her grandmother, Princess Augusta, Duchess of Cambridge, had brought a lilac tree from Schloss Rumpenheim, her home in Germany, and planted it in the garden of Cambridge Cottage, Kew in 1838. Princess May successfully transplanted the tree to Frogmore where it continues to flourish. After the long quiet years of Queen Victoria's reign Princess May and her family brought a refreshing note of youth to Frogmore, and while the children went boating on the lake, explored the limitless mysteries of the grounds or looked after their own little gardens, the Princess could enjoy the soothing atmosphere of the old house.

After the Prince of Wales became King George V and Windsor Castle became their official residence, Queen Mary never lost her affection for Frogmore and continued to visit the grounds whenever possible. Inherent

Opposite: Queen Victoria's Indian kiosk: "exquisite oriental symmetry"

in her love of gardens was a dislike of untidiness and during the inter-war years she turned her attention to organizing the clearing of some of the shrubberies at Frogmore, which had become dense jungles smothering much of the original beauty. One of Queen Mary's great pleasures must have been clearing away the thick binds of ivy, her perpetual enemy in any garden, as Osbert Sitwell describes in *Queen Mary and Others*. In place of some of the laurel and yew trees appeared flowering cherries and syringas and the old ponticum rhododendrons were cut back to a manageable size. But during the Second World War the work lapsed and, as in the Savill Gardens, the enforced neglect was exacerbated by the winter of 1946–47 when floods covered much of the gardens.

Since the last War the house at Frogmore has not been used regularly and in some of the rooms are the various Royal possessions which Queen Mary affectionately collected together to form her Royal museum. But because of the limited privacy of Windsor Castle and the short journey to them from London the grounds have continued to be the retreat Queen Charlotte originally intended. To this end Queen Victoria captured what has always been their appeal when she wrote in 1867, 'I am sitting in this dear lovely garden, where *all* is Peace and quiet and you can only hear the hum of the bees, the singing of the birds and the occasional crowing and cackling from the Poultry Yard! It does my poor excited, worried nerves – good!'

Today Frogmore's grounds present a picture of unspoilt and, in many parts, unchanged continuity with the past. In recent years far more extensive clearance of the dense shrubberies has been carried out, and rather than causing the old features of the gardens to disappear the new work is preserving the essential landscape. Part of the new programmes are the long border along the south end of the grounds, and the border leading away from the house towards the Gothic ruins. Particularly along the long south boundary the clearance has opened up the grounds considerably, but in a few years the new shrubs, mainly syringas and shrub roses, will mature to provide a more colourful screen than the old evergreen laurels and yews.

Another area of new planting, commemorating Queen Elizabeth II's Silver Jubilee in 1977, is the mound which stretches down to Queen Victoria's little tea-house. The majority of the new plants here were obtained with a donation made to The Queen by the National Gardens Scheme to celebrate the Jubilee. The area will add great seasonal variety to the grounds, for it has been designed as a winter garden whose differing shades of leaf and flower will add a cheering note to the emptier months. Among the various new plants are a number of evergreen *Mahonias* whose yellow flowers often have a distinctive scent, Witch Hazels (*Hamamelis*) and dwarf conifers, and around the shrubs clusters of delicate winter aconites and snowdrops.

The winter garden is a good example of how the recent planting is

Queen Victoria's Tea House

carefully blended with the old features and character of the grounds. In particular, the retention of the old beech trees and a number of forsythias, holly and yew trees, preserves the distinctly Victorian feeling in this part of the grounds. Elsewhere clearings, balanced with careful preservation of trees, are the basis of Frogmore's appearance in the spring and early summer when the grounds as a whole are at their best. Where old shrubs and thickets have been removed the ground has been grassed over and planted with thousands of bulbs, so that the beeches, planes, chestnuts and oaks regain their varying shades of foliage above glorious displays of daffodils, snowdrops, primroses and polyanthus. Behind Queen Victoria and Prince Albert's mausoleum work is beginning on a new spring garden, where the cleared ground will be rejuvenated with Spanish bluebells, primroses and forsythias.

Queen Charlotte always intended the grounds of Frogmore to contain both beauty and botanical interest, and the continuation of this ideal is perhaps reflected most by the exceptionally fine trees to be found there. In particular their combination with the wide lawns and the intangible magic of the lake's reflections, seen from whatever angle, presents a scene whose picturesque appearance was Major Price's ultimate goal. Venerable cedars and oaks, including two gnarled and ancient holm oaks, shade the lawns, while in contrast the narrow, towering Incense Cedar still stands between the house and the island, having survived, so it is reported, its topmost branches being thinned out when King George V accidentally shot it, and also being struck by lightning a few years ago. Rising from the edges of the lake are majestic planes, and two Swamp Cypresses (*Taxodium disticum*) which thrive on the saturated soil; the island contains an element of surprise: its narrow path leads mysteriously between thick rhododendrons and laurels to emerge beneath open stands of beech and chestnut. The canopies of luxuriant chestnuts also protect the flowering cherries on the slope, carpeted with daffodils in spring, which leads up to the Duchess of Kent's mausoleum. Standing beside the mausoleum is an unusually large Strawberry Tree, whose evergreen leaves are filled in autumn with white flowers and red strawberry-like fruits. At the far end of the lake, near the blue-shaded Bhutan Pine, are two smaller flowering trees – a Tulip Tree, and a *Magnolia hypoleuca* planted by King George V in 1935 to commemorate the Silver Jubilee of his accession.

Among Frogmore's most intriguing features are the thick bunches of mistletoe which fill the upper branches of the many lime trees in the grounds, and which were once described, somewhat comically, in an account of the gardens, as rooks' nests. Among the most unusual possessions is the mulberry avenue on the opposite side of the house from the garden front. The gnarled old fruit trees flank the road leading from the main entrance of the house across the Home Park to Prince Albert's dairy.

As has been seen with the matters of clearance and new planting, much of Frogmore's success and continuing health derive from the balance between continuity and change. This is clearly shown in the area to the north-east of the lawn in front of the house. The path crosses the little bridge over this narrow end of the lake and passes the Gothic ruins, beyond which the rose garden and lawns lead to the Indian kiosk. Wyatt's ruins have achieved the reality of antiquity and over the walls Chinese and Japanese wisterias trail their mauve and violet strands like the hair of old men. The rose garden replaced Queen Charlotte's little Dutch garden, whose pattern of low hedges and flower-beds became uncontrollably overgrown; but although the beds were originally filled with hybrid tea and floribundae varieties, these have recently been replaced by older shrub roses far more in keeping with the Victorian influence of that part of the grounds.

With the wonderfully decorative language which fills his essay, *On The Making Of Gardens*, Sir George Sitwell describes in one passage the beauty and quality of age in a garden, which is very applicable to Frogmore: 'Restfulness is the prevailing note of an old garden; in this fairy world of echo and suggestion where the Present never comes but to commune with the Past . . . How few there are who are incapable of feeling the mysterious appeal of such a place – of the scenes which reflect upon us the passion and happiness of bygone generations . . . It is this harmony with the surroundings which we feel upon entering an old house or garden; vague ancestral memories are faintly stirred and the sentiment which may attach to objects that have been habitual sources of enjoyment to generation after generation.' Frogmore's grounds abound with a sense of the past and the influence of members of the Royal Family who for generations have enjoyed it as a sanctuary from the pressures of their public life. The view from the colonnade of Queen Charlotte's house, across the lawns and past willows and cedars towards the lake, has changed little in nearly two centuries. Princess Elizabeth's Hermitage still peeps from between trees and the windows of Queen Victoria's tea-house look out onto the young plants of her great-great-grandaughter's Jubilee winter garden. Among the trees, memorials to Lady Augusta Stanley, lady-in-waiting to the Duchess of Kent, to John Brown, Queen Victoria's sturdy Highland servant and to Princess Beatrice's – Queen Victoria's youngest child – little dog Wat, speak of past service and gratitude. Added to the serenity of the old Georgian house is the particular mystique which the mausoleum of Queen Victoria and Prince Albert gives the surroundings and the rare quality of its landscape, which are the secret of Frogmore's continuing, if fadingly nostalgic attraction.

WINDSOR CASTLE

Berkshire

IN TERMS OF ANTIQUITY AND GRANDEUR all the Royal houses, palaces and castles, past and present, pale beside Windsor. No other residence has been used by every English monarch as Windsor Castle has since the Conqueror erected the original wooden building, looking north over steep cliffs to the valley of the Thames, one of his circle of fortresses built around London to guard the town in the years immediately after 1066. But while those at Hertford, Tochester, Tonbridge, Guildford and other strategic positions are in ruins or survive only in part, Windsor continued to be enlarged and altered by successive generations of kings. Its role as castle and palace, with forbidding towers surrounded by leafy gardens and joined by sumptuous apartments, is unique; and its aura derives from the image of supreme power dominating the archetypal English setting, which inspired Samuel Pepys to describe it in 1666 as, 'The most romantique Castle that is in the world,' and Thomas Gray to write a hundred years later:

> 'From the stately brow
> Of Windsor's heights, the expanse below
> Of grove, of lawn, of mead, survey,
> Whose turf, whose shade, whose flowers among,
> Wanders the hoary Thames along
> His silver winding way.'

The original castle was built of wood because of the need for haste in construction; it was of the traditional Norman plan of upper and lower wards, divided by a high mound on which stood the central tower, or keep, of the castle (at Windsor, the Round Tower). The Conqueror and his son

Opposite : Part of the Moat Garden with the Dean's House beyond

used the stronghold principally as a prison, and here William Rufus imprisoned Robert, Earl of Northumbria, for thirty years, after the latter's rebellion in 1095. But by the beginning of the twelfth century Henry I, William I's scholarly younger son had built the first Royal chambers in the upper ward where the present State Apartments are sited; and it was in his new chapel within the castle that he married his Queen, Adeline, in 1121.

The turmoil of the Civil War between Henry I's daughter, Athelic, or Matilda, and her cousin Stephen, was only brought to order by the accession in 1154 of Henry II, Matilda's son and the first Plantagenet King. Henry II began the replacement of the wooden framework of the castle with stone and established the first gardens; in 1156 and 1158 respectively he was recorded to have a vineyard and orchard outside the south wall of the castle. By his death in 1189 Henry II had virtually completed surrounding the castle with stonework; inside he had built the Great Hall in the lower ward and the *Domus Regis* or 'King's house' in the upper. Part of these buildings formed a square cloister which may have contained a herb garden for his Queen, Eleanor of Aquitaine, whose apartments were along the west side of the cloister.

Henry II's work at Windsor is of great interest because it is a clear example of the twelfth-century transition from a tradition of wooden fortresses, hurriedly put up for defensive purposes, to one of more permanent stone buildings which were secure and therefore more suited to a settled life. The annual records of the vines planted in his extensive vineyards and of the grapes harvested are evidence of the growing domestic side to life in the castle. The homes which Henry developed enthusiastically in other parts of England also contained gardens, and at the old Royal palace of Woodstock he is reputed to have planted a labyrinth or maze, in the centre of which, hidden by the tall hedges from discovery by his wife, he seduced his mistress, Rosamund Clifford.

Though Henry II's orchards and vineyards showed that simple gardens were beginning to play a part in medieval life, further fortification of the castle was always the main priority of his work at Windsor. Not until the reign of his grandson, Henry III, was attention once again turned to the beautification of the Royal Chambers. Only nine years old at the end of John's turbulent reign in 1216, Henry became a man of as great culture as his Plantagenet forebears, and his work at Windsor set the scene for the future glories of Edward III's reign and for the foundation of the Order of the Garter, through which the castle continues to hold alive the mystique of medieval chivalry.

Henry III must be credited with giving Windsor its first pleasure gardens which were devised for the enjoyment of his wife, Eleanor of Provence, a lady of sophisticated background. The windows of the Queen's apartments, which Henry ordered to be filled with glass because of the contrast between the climates of Windsor and her native Mediterranean, were recorded to be 'facing on to the King's herb garden' where a lawn was also laid, probably planted with small flowers. Here the Queen could walk in privacy or, from her rooms, look out on to the secluded beauty of the cloister or 'garth'. When the Queen's apartments were extended, they were built in what was becoming the typical medieval plan, around a second cloister or herb garden.

Henry's piety inspired him to rebuild Westminster Abbey and at Windsor to build a small chapel to the memory of Edward the Confessor in the lower ward of the castle. On the north side of the chapel a cloister surrounded a plot of grass, which survives today and is held to be the oldest lawn in England: it is now part of the Dean's Cloister. Outside the castle walls Henry improved his grandfather's original vineyards and orchard garden by enclosing them with hedges and adding a shrubbery, wells and a stone fountain. During the years of Henry's long reign Windsor was transformed by his projects, the pursuit of which often rendered him penniless, and at one time forced him to pawn the castle's most valued treasure, a gilt statue of the Virgin Mary, the 'Virgin of Windsor'. His work reflected a major contribution to the evolution of England – and the monarchy – from the aggressive feudalism of the Norman and early Plantagenet reigns to the zenith of the English Middle Ages, the reign of Edward III.

Edward III bestowed upon Windsor its most prestigious possession, the Order of the Garter. Founded as a brotherhood of Knights of Saint George in 1348, comprising the King, Edward, Prince of Wales, (the Black Prince) and twenty-four knights, the Order embodied the heroic and pious qualities of chivalry that blossomed during Edward III's reign; and still today Windsor's martial atmosphere is perhaps more evocative of this period than of any other. Edward celebrated the establishment of Windsor as the home of the Order by erecting new buildings for its canons to the north of the chapel on the site of Henry III's apartments, which had been destroyed by fire in 1295. He also embarked on rebuilding and expanding the apartments of the upper ward, preserving the old pattern and thus retaining the two cloister gardens.

While these works were progressing Edward and his Queen Philippa, lived in the Round Tower, and it is probable that the Moat Garden of today dates from that time; it has changed little in appearance in the ensuing six hundred years. The moat had always been dry, and in 1319 it was recorded that five women were each paid a penny a day for mowing *kumphos* and nettles for two days. Thus the slopes and valley of the moat were at times kept tidy, but it is most likely that Edward III's decision to use the old keep of the castle for domestic purposes led to the appearance of the first gardens. We can be certain that the garden existed by the beginning of the fifteenth century thanks to the works of two poets, James I of Scotland and Geoffrey Chaucer.

James I was unfortunate enough to be captured at sea in 1405 when only a child, and upon Henry V's accession in 1413 he was moved to

Windsor, where he was treated with great respect and given a liberal education, living in rooms in the Devil's Tower – traditionally a prison – which overlooked the south side of the moat. Still confined in 1423, James wrote *The Kingis Quair* – Quair meaning book – which tells of his adoration of Lady Jane Beaufort, daughter of the Duke of Somerset and grandaughter of John of Gaunt, who upon James's release became his wife and returned with him to Scotland. In the poem James tells how he first saw Lady Jane walking in the moat garden and immediately fell in love with her, describing the garden in vivid and charming detail:

> 'Now was there made, fast by the tower's wall
> A garden fair, and in the corners set
> An herb'ry green, with wandes long and small
> Railed about, and so with trees beset
> Was all the place, and hawthorn hedges knit,
> That life was none, walking there forebye
> That might within scarce any wight espy.
>
> So thick the boughs, and the leaves green
> Beshaded all the alleys that there were,
> And 'midst every arbour might be seen
> The sharp, green, sweet junipers
> Growing so fair, with branches here and there,
> That, as it seemed to a life without,
> The boughs spread the arbours all about
>
> And on the small green twiggies sat
> The little sweet nightingale, and song
> So loud and clear the hymnis consecrate
> Of love his use, now soft, now loud among
> That all the gardens and the walls rung
> Right of their song.'

The poet goes on to describe how he saw Lady Jane walking in the idyllic setting:

> ... 'Whereas I saw, walking under the tower
> Full secretly, now coming her to pleyn,
> The fairest and the freshest younge floure
> That ever I saw, methought, before that hour ...'

The young Scottish King was an admirer of Chaucer's work, which also contains probable references to Windsor. Chaucer was an adoring servant of Princess Joan, the beautiful wife of the Black Prince and legendary 'Fair Maid of Kent' whose dropped garter is traditionally believed to have inspired the naming of the Order. In 1390 her son, Richard II, appointed Chaucer Clerk of the Works to restore the chapel of St George, and it is easy to believe that Chaucer used the Round Tower and the moat garden as the setting for the famous passage in *The Knight's Tale* when Palamon, imprisoned in the great tower, first sees Emilie gathering flowers in the garden below. Chaucer describes the flowers which Emilie picked as red and white, soon to be the conflicting badges of the Wars of the Roses – the red rose of the House of Lancaster and the white rose of the House of York.

The original garden and vineyards planted by Henry II outside the castle walls were over three hundred years old when Edward IV – who emerged victorious from the Wars of the Roses as the first Yorkist King – drew special attention to them during the visit of a foreign nobleman. Edward was entertaining Seigneur de la Gruthuyse from Holland and, despite not returning from hunting until very late on one particular day, the King insisted on showing his guest the garden and vineyards which had become features of importance and repute. Edward IV's major contribution to Windsor was the present St George's Chapel, which he began building in the 1470s, adjoining the west end of Henry III's original chapel. His inspired work was possibly spurred on by the view from the castle of Eton College Chapel built by his predecessor and Lancastrian rival, Henry VI; and although the new chapel was not finished at Edward's death, only the choir being ready, it was brought to spectacular completion during Henry VII's reign with the addition of the nave and the vaulted ceilings.

By the reign of Henry VII the eastern half of the Moat Garden had been replaced by a wooden tennis court where King Philip of Castile played when visiting Henry in 1506 to be installed as a Knight of the Garter. The tennis court was popular with Henry VIII (who also built the one at Hampton Court); and the Earl of Surrey recorded wistfully during his imprisonment at Windsor how the ladies used to watch the play from the battlements above. One important addition during Henry VIII's reign was the original North Terrace, put up in 1533 and made of wood, which replaced the narrow path that had previously stretched below the windows of the Royal apartments. A bridge carried the terrace over the ditch at the eastern end to a new arbour painted in the Tudor colours of green and white and possibly similar to the King's Great Round Arbour at Hampton Court. The idea of a terrace leading in this manner to an arbour, where wandering courtiers could rest or take refreshment, can be seen as an early forerunner of the scheme which became widespread in the later seventeenth and eighteenth centuries, of an *allée* between hedges, or avenue leading to a temple, grotto or some other point of rest or interest. The terrace was rebuilt and improved by Henry's daughter, Elizabeth I.

Despite the pageantry of the Garter ceremonies of Henry VIII's reign, the addition of the new gateway to the lower ward and his development of the North Terrace, memories of these years are tarnished by the deaths of the three Windsor Martyrs who were burnt at the stake in the Chapter Garden below the north slopes in 1544. Even the reign of Henry's daughter, Mary Tudor, notorious for its religious persecutions, did not witness any such deeds at Windsor. In contrast, Mary's visits to Windsor provided her with some of the few happy times in her reign. Here she proclaimed her husband, Philip II of Spain, joint-sovereign in 1554, after their marriage at Winchester. And in 1555 a scheme begun during the short reign of Edward VI – the piping of water to the castle from Blackmore Park five miles away – was successfully completed when the pipe was brought to the centre of the Quadrangle in the upper ward. Here it was adorned in a style typical of the period and reminiscent of much of Henry VIII's decoration of Hampton Court, with a fountain elaborately made up of, 'a canopy raised upon columns, gorgeously decorated with heraldic ornaments coloured and gilt, and a dragon, one of the supporters of the Tudor arms, casting the water into the basin underneath'.

Numerous pictures of Tudor, and in particular, of Elizabethan Windsor are contained in Shakespeare's work, the best-known being in *The Merry Wives of Windsor*, recorded as being first performed in the castle in front of Elizabeth I. During Elizabeth I's reign it became obvious that her father's wooden North Terrace was rotting, and in 1582 it was replaced with a wide stone terrace deemed more fitting as the dividing line between the castle buildings and the steep slopes down to the Thames valley. In 1598 Paul Hentzner described the terrace as, 'a walk of incredible beauty, three hundred and eighty paces in length'. The terrace, leading to the Little Park, satisfied Elizabeth's demand for exercise and enjoyment of walking as did, with different surroundings, the relatively new gardens at Hampton Court. In the Little Park an elm avenue planted by William III was always named after Elizabeth I, perhaps because it lay on the site of one of her favourite walks. During the sixteenth century, when other Royal palaces such as Hampton Court and Greenwich were being adorned for the Royal pleasure, Windsor Castle's role was to embody in comparison the traditional citadel of Royal power. The changes that took place then can be seen as attempts to ensure the preservation and if necessary the improvement of this state. Within and around the castle the gardens remained largely unchanged for, unlike Hampton Court, whose buildings and gardens were a conscious symbol of Tudor taste and splendour, Windsor's atmosphere of strength from long establishment clearly demanded to be preserved.

For seventeen years during the Civil War the sovereign lost control of Windsor Castle for the only time since the Middle Ages and, like the rest of the country, it was garrisoned by the Parliamentary armies. Windsor was Charles I's last place of imprisonment before he was taken to St James's Palace the day before his execution in 1649. His body was returned to St George's Chapel, where it lies in a vault with Henry VIII and his favourite Queen, Jane Seymour. The Restoration of 1660 returned the castle to its rightful owner amidst scenes of euphoric joy. It also heralded a number of changes reflecting the influence that exile in France had had upon Charles II, as his projects at Hampton Court and the other Royal palaces also showed. The north front of the upper ward at Windsor was transformed, outside by new buildings with a regular façade and tall

Italianate windows, and inside with ceilings painted by Verrio and carvings by Grinling Gibbons. But despite the changes the basic form of the buildings was preserved, and the two small cloister gardens survived to be renamed Brick Court and Horn Court.

Although the situation of the castle left limited scope for extensive gardens within the immediate vicinity of the buildings, the filling in of the ditch which had previously enclosed the east and south fronts of the upper ward was a major transformation. It allowed for the extension of the North Terrace along the east and part of the south fronts, thus aiding the visual unity between the buildings and the surrounding parkland. John Evelyn, whose detailed records of the Royal activities of the period describe elsewhere the changes at Hampton Court, wrote of Windsor in 1683: 'There was now the *Terraces* almost brought round the old *Castle*' (referring to the upper ward), 'The Grass made clean, even and curiously turf't, also the *Avenues* to the New-Park, and other Walkes planted with *Elmes* and limes, and a pretty Canale, and receptacle for fowle.' It was at this time that the east terrace was first extended, and beyond the terrace a new bowling-green was laid out.

In 1684, after purchasing the necessary land for £1200, Charles II began the planting of the most impressive addition to the castle's surroundings – the avenue which came in Queen Anne's reign to be called the 'Long Walk'. The elm trees stretched away from the south front to the top of Snow Hill three miles off in the Great Park; this had the effect of opening up the inward-looking security the castle had always seemed happy to enjoy behind its high walls and gateways. The Long Walk was Charles II's legacy to Windsor of a style, inspired by le Nôtre, which he developed in more detail at his other palaces, but which at Windsor he was content to indulge with one majestic vista.

The name of André le Nôtre, however, was to recur at Windsor during the reign of William and Mary. William intended to transform Windsor at the hand of Sir Christopher Wren, as he did Hampton Court. Wren had become the architect at Windsor during Charles II's reign, and when William revealed ambitions to revolutionize the castle's appearance Wren presented the King with plans that would have turned it into a romantic dream in the Italian style. Part of the plan was the new appearance of the north front, which was to be broken by lower terraces looking on to formal gardens leading down to the river. These gardens were to be the work of le Nôtre who, though eighty-five, still retained his unrivalled reputation. He also appears to have agreed to the task, as in 1698 William Bentinck, the first Earl of Portland, wrote to the King from France: 'M. le Nôtre will make me a plan for the gardens contemplated at Windsor.' But, as with the plans for Wren's north front at Hampton Court, luckily the project came to nothing because of prohibitive cost; and the medieval character of the castle was allowed to survive.

From Charles II's reign the area of the Little Park below the north terrace was always known as 'Maestricht'. The name derived from the capture in 1694 of the ancient Dutch fortress of Maestricht by the armies of Charles II and Louis XIV of France during the Third Dutch War. The victory was celebrated by Charles II at Windsor with a reconstruction of the siege in which the Duke of Monmouth and Duke of York stormed the fortress, to the delight of the spectators. William III's plans for gardens came to nought, but they were revived by his sister-in-law, Queen Anne, for whom Windsor was second to none as a favourite home; though even after her accession Queen Anne retained the small red brick house opposite the old Rubbish Gate in the south front which she had bought from Lord Godolphin when William and Mary were inhabiting the castle, and throughout her reign seemed to prefer the small-scale domesticity of the villa and adjoining gardens to the grandeur of the state apartments in the castle.

Part of Queen Anne's affection for Windsor derived from her zealous enjoyment of stag hunting, and her head-gardener, Henry Wise, was kept continually busy laying out rides and roads in the park, along which the Queen could hurtle in her chaise. Agnes Strickland wrote: 'In this extraordinary and dangerous hunting equipage she was known to drive her fine strong hackney forty or fifty miles on a summer's afternoon ... Notwithstanding the straight avenues in which the chases and forests of France are cut, likewise those of Hampton Court and Windsor to imitate them, the chaise hunting of Anne and the phaeton hunting of the French kings and their courts remain to us historical mysteries.' Anne's hunting exploits are preserved for memory at Windsor by Queen Anne's Ride, an avenue which runs for three miles through the park from Queen Anne's Gate to the Prince Consort's Gate. She was also responsible for making the road along Charles II's great avenue, from which time the avenue took on the name of the Long Walk.

Shortly after Anne's accession Wise's attention was turned from the gardens that he had made for the Queen at Kensington Palace and the chaise-rides in Windsor Park, to the far more testing task of taking up William III's plans for gardens on the site of Maestricht. The riverside area was subject to regular flooding and the gardens, unfinished at Anne's death, did not long survive her, gradually disappearing beneath the parkland from which they had emerged. But during her reign the Queen persisted with her ambitions, and a canal was dug, surrounded by clipped yew and fruit trees laid out in formal patterns, which must have presented a startling contrast between the North Terrace and the natural wooded riverbank which they temporarily replaced. The Maestricht project was probably the most ambitious garden attempted at Windsor by any monarch, and the measure of success enjoyed reflected both the tenacity of Queen Anne and the talents of the faithful Henry Wise.

As the Maestricht gardens disappeared so use of the castle by the monarchy went into decline during the reigns of George I and George II,

The south side of the Moat Garden, overlooked by the Devil's Tower, where the young King James I of Scotland was imprisoned

and many parts fell into a state of considerable disrepair. Not until the reign of George III were any of the badly-needed improvements begun. A visit to Windsor for the Garter ceremony in 1762 revealed that many of the state rooms were virtually uninhabitable, and much of the east and south fronts were taken up with grace-and-favour apartments. But both King George III and Queen Charlotte developed an affection for the old castle, enchanted by its atmosphere and by the surrounding parks, which offered potential scope for the King to experiment with the various agricultural plans that were so dear to him. From 1776 they took over the house which Queen Anne had lived in below the south front (which was enlarged and came to be called the Queen's Lodge) and Burford House nearby, which had been built by Charles II for Nell Gwyn (which was now called the Lower Lodge). Here the Royal Family came for the weeks of the summer while repairs were begun in the castle. The gardens of the two houses adjoined each other, and the Queen was happy to spend her time here with her daughters, while the King was often at the new Royal Dairy or one of his two new farms in the Great Park, Norwich and Flemish farms (whose names derived from the farming systems being modelled on the two original areas).

Although the Royal Family did not take possession of the new apartments in the castle until 1804 their visits to the Queen's Lodge involved active interest in the castle and its surroundings. On the slopes below the North Terrace which led down to the site of Queen Anne's gardens in Maestricht, the King and Queen began making 'pleasure grounds' of which one feature – The Temple of Fame – survives in the present Home Park. The Temple of Fame originated in the King's enthusiasm for the Gothic revival. It was an intriguing flint cave full of niches and entered by winding passages, and an example of the fashion for grottos, widespread in the later eighteenth century, that was begun by Alexander Pope with the grotto at his villa at Twickenham. The niches were supposed originally to have been designed for busts of past famous British naval and military leaders, although they do not survive today.

The early alterations to the castle begun by George III sadly included the disappearance of the oldest gardens below the walls of the south front. Having survived for over six hundred years the garden and vineyards begun by Henry II were finally destroyed when the last remaining stretch of the medieval ditch was filled in around 1780, down to the Henry VIII gateway. However, the medieval presence survived in the Moat Garden where the part that had originally been the tennis court and subsequently a barracks was levelled in. Charles Knight, who lived in Windsor and was later to write a detailed guide to the castle, remembered playing in the Moat Garden in the early days of George III's reign.

During George III's reign the North Terrace saw scenes of great social activity when the King and Queen were at Windsor. In the evening they walked along the terrace amongst the crowds who assembled to see

them, in an atmosphere of informality between King and people which was very much a characteristic of his reign. But by the latter years of his reign this and other activities at Windsor, including Wyatt's reconstruction of the upper ward in the Gothic style, had stopped, and the sad figure of the King was confined to his rooms on the north wing owing to his blindness and supposed insanity, now generally believed to have been porphyria – a belief supported by the present Prince of Wales, who has done a great deal to redress posterity's unfair labelling of George III as insane. For far from being a form of lunacy, as was diagnosed to be the King's affliction by his contemporaries, porphyria is primarily a physical illness, involving a swelling of glands which brings on extreme abdominal pain and resultant bouts of mental disorder. This would account for the intermittent nature of the King's illness until the latter years of his reign, alternating with periods of complete mental clarity. A famous, if possibly apocryphal story, relates to a scene which occurred at Windsor and which was recorded by one of the King's pages, Philip Withers. One day when Withers was with the King and Queen riding in the park, the page witnessed the King dismount from his horse and, to the astonished alarm of the Queen, shake a branch of an oak tree as he would shake the hand of a friend, and talk to the tree in all earnestness, convinced that he was talking to the King of Prussia. As a result of his doctors' diagnosis of insanity the King suffered great hardship, for their usual remedy was to force him into a strait waistcoat until his periods of disorder subsided.

The castle itself was never a home for Queen Charlotte, as Kew and Frogmore were, and this, along with the fact that the worst scenes of the King's illness took place within its walls, explains why her great interest in gardening and botany did not have a lasting effect on the castle gardens. As is described elsewhere Frogmore was where the Queen was happiest and where she was able to enjoy her love of horticulture, though from 1804 there were periods when she was in residence at Windsor in her new apartments in the Queen's Tower on the corner of the east and south fronts. The Queen's Tower has contained the rooms of every Queen since Queen Charlotte, save only George IV's luckless wife, Queen Catherine.

Shortly after his accession King George IV decided to continue the Gothic reconstruction of the upper ward on a far more extensive scale than was probably ever envisaged by his father. The work was entrusted to Jeffry Wyatt (later to assume the name of Wyatville), whose plans were chosen in preference to those of a number of other architects. Wyatville was the nephew of James Wyatt, King George III's architect. The work was not completed during George IV's reign – the last project, the Royal Mews, was finished in 1842 – and was fantastically expensive. The original amount agreed by Parliament for the buildings and interior decorations and furniture was £300,000, but the final cost was reckoned to have been nearer £1,000,000.

The striking effect of the exterior of the new buildings, and the splendour of the interiors, transformed the upper ward and gave Windsor the overwhelming grandeur which it enjoys today. Queen Charlotte's apartments had been on the corner of the east and south fronts but George IV was the first King to use the east front for the Royal private apartments, where they have continued to be ever since, leaving the north front free to become the State apartments. The south front had apartments for guests, and Wyatville joined it to the east front with the enormous Grand Corridor, 250 feet long, along the inside of the two fronts.

One of Wyatville's greatest additions to Windsor, the King George IV Gateway, which replaced the Rubbish Gate as the entrance to the upper ward from the south, necessitated demolition of the Queen's Lodge and the house's gardens. This was compensated for by the seemingly limitless vista of the Long Walk, unbroken except by the road to Frogmore on to which the huge arch of the gateway opened. In 1821 the King ordered an equestrian statue of his father, pointing towards the castle, to be erected upon the distant Snow Hill to crown the view. The enormous statue, known as 'The Copper Horse' was made by Sir Richard Westmacott and

A coloured drawing by
Edward Wells, with
Queen Victoria and
Prince Albert on the
balcony of the Queen's
Tower and the Royal
children on the terrace
below, looking from the
south side of the castle
to the East Terrace
Garden as originally laid
out by Wyatville

placed upon an equally gigantic base made by Wyatville. Not only did the
figure derive from the famous equestrian statue of Marcus Aurelius in
the Capitoline Piazza in Rome, but Wyatville's base, in the 'Picturesque'
style of the period, was given a partially ruined appearance, feigning
antiquity, by the rough boulders strewn around it as though it were
crumbling away. The whole construction stands over 50 feet high, and
belittles the distance of three miles to the castle.

The positioning of the King's apartments along the east front led
Wyatville to replace Charles II's old bowling-green with the fitting

formality of the present East Terrace Garden, sunk below a broad terrace
and wall which divided it from the Little Park, still open to the public.
This, with the Moat Garden, is today the main garden within the castle
and still largely private. The bay windows between the four towers –
Prince of Wales Tower, Chester Tower, Clarence Tower and the Queen's
Tower – looked out on to a view of majestic but simple design
complementing the architecture with its regular pattern.

Wyatville's East Terrace Garden was principally designed to contain

the various statues and vases which George IV had brought to Windsor, mainly from Hampton Court. These ornaments were arranged around the sunken terrace, whose lawns were divided by wide paths at right-angles. The centrepiece of the plan were the pool and fountain which remain today. The fountain was originally surmounted by a bronze figure of Hercules and Acalus in the form of a snake, which was made for George IV, but this was subsequently removed to Kew. Around most of the sunken garden slopes lead down from the wide encircling path, but along the north side Wyatville built the 300 foot-long Orangery, lit by high windows, which originally housed thirty-four orange trees given to George IV by Charles X, the last Bourbon King of France.

Wyatville's laying-out of the East Terrace Garden was the last major structural alteration or addition to the gardens within the walls of the castle, and since the beginning of the nineteenth century his terrace and the Moat Garden have been the two largest areas at Windsor. The limited space of the gardens prompted Prince Albert during the 1840s to organize a major contribution to the privacy of the Royal Family when at Windsor – the development of the five hundred acres of the Little Park into the present Home Park. The Little Park had been open to the public, encircled by a road which led to the old Datchet bridge from both directions, while another road passed straight by Frogmore, as well as being crossed by a public footpath. Despite containing some outstanding old trees the appearance of the park in general was somewhat unkempt. By the time of the Prince Consort's death the road had been diverted, the now tidy fields of the park – private from 1851 – were crossed by a series of new avenues leading to various destinations, and the Royal Family were able to visit Frogmore, Adelaide Cottage or the new model dairy undisturbed.

During the nineteenth century the old Moat Garden was largely neglected, but from 1901 it was transformed by General Sir Dighton Probyn, who had been appointed Keeper of the Privy Purse by King Edward VII and lived in the house beside the Norman Gateway. Sir Dighton filled the crescent-shaped moat and steep slopes of the mound with numerous flowers, shrubs and garden ornaments so that the Round Tower rose up out of deep beds of colour. The small size of the garden was offset by its unusual shape which gave scope for the great variety which filled the limited space. Around the base of the moat ran a brick path, called the Lavender Walk, with vases of lavender at intervals on either side, and below the high outside wall of the moat stretched a long narrow herbaceous border. Inside the path were other beds filled with roses and tulips for spring colour, and small lawns whose different levels were joined by flights of low steps. Shading the lawns were a variety of trees, some of which, like the walnut tree, are still there, being of considerable age.

Above the moat the steep sides of the mound were broken up by terraces and adjoining paths and steps like a miniature Italian garden.

Previous page: Looking across the East Terrace Garden
a) south-east to the Home Park
b) towards the east front of the castle with the Warwick Vase copy at the foot of the steps leading down to the garden

From the south-east end of the moat a metal pergola swathed in clematis and climbing roses covered the flight of steps which led to the Fountain Terrace. Metal arbours covered with more clematis and roses stretched across the terrace which curved for about thirty yards around the side of the mound. From the Fountain Terrace the path continued up the slope and led to King James's Herbere in the uppermost northern corner of the garden, a little garden-house named after the young Scottish King who centuries earlier had gazed out of the windows of his prison into the garden below. Most of the slopes of the mound were broken by little terraces filled with shrubs and plants, but below the Herbere the bank was left unbroken and filled with daffodil bulbs. Close by, Sir Dighton Probyn made a rockery with the same Norfolk car-stone used around the lakes in the gardens of Sandringham, covering the stones with a variety of alpines. Below the rockery a water garden tumbled into the north-eastern end of the moat.

As a result of Sir Dighton's work the Moat Garden, ingeniously designed and so filled with plants that there hardly seemed to be any empty space left, became an oasis of bloom and blossom in the centre of the surrounding stone walls of the castle. Sir Dighton's successors in the Norman Tower-house have ensured the maintenance of the garden and made a number of alterations; since 1964 the house has been the residence of the Constable and Governor of the castle. The changes have been mainly to the contents of the garden, so that during this century its character has remained unaltered, and reminiscent of the garden which the Scottish King James described over five hundred years ago. The note of variety which Sir Dighton gave is still very evident in the number of trees which shade the lawns and stretch out from the slopes above. As well as the old walnut and an even older mulberry tree, there are flowering cherries; and a crab-apple tree which may survive from the early nineteenth century when the moat was filled with fruit trees; a 'Judas Tree' covered with delicate lilac-coloured flowers in May, a 'Strawberry Tree'; and an unusual pomegranate which thrives on the warmth of the south-facing slope and gives an exotic display of scarlet funnel-shaped flowers in late summer.

At the south-east end of the moat, near the doorway in the outside south wall, there is an area which has the appearance of a garden within a garden. In the outer wall is an alcove called 'Poets' Corner', whose walls are covered with quotations from the verses of Queen Victoria's Poet Laureate, Tennyson, (to whom it is dedicated) and other versifiers. Poets' Corner looks out onto a miniature rose-garden and a magnificent stone well-head whose four corners are surmounted by lead figures of lions, over which a metal arbour supports a canopy of climbing roses. From here the path and lawns of the moat curve away, flanked as in Sir Dighton Probyn's time, by a narrow border below the outer wall and roses on the inside. Trained to the stonework of the high outer wall are climbing roses, a

Magnolia (*grandiflora*) and a syringa. King James's Herbere remains perched above the daffodil bank, the rockery and water-garden where a stone hippopotamus's head gurgles water into one of the stone baths at the base of the cascade; but the pergola and arbours over the Fountain Terrace have gone. The high platform of the terrace looks out over St George's Chapel and the lower ward of the castle; and in the low retaining wall behind is the lead lion's-head water-spout, which gave Fountain Terrace its name, over a large lead water-butt dated 1781 and carved with classical figures. Among the plants which cling to the terraces of the mound slopes are hydrangeas below King James's Herbere, and on the south side below the Judas Tree, clusters of pink nerines. From this side of the garden, where steps lead up to the fig-tree arbour, there are wonderful views of the distant park stretching away from the buildings below the south walls of the castle.

Ever since Sir Dighton Probyn originally planned its re-organization nearly one hundred years ago the Moat Garden has continued to defy the limitations of its size and the problems presented by the steep slopes which from their highest point drop 90 feet to the bottom of the moat. And despite the changes, the lawns and trees of the moat, surrounded as they always have been by the walls and towers of the castle, conjure up thoughts of the medieval days when the garden was first made for the ladies of the court. Today, visitors to the castle can look from the walls down into the curving garden shaped like a miniature amphitheatre, as the Tudor courtiers did when watching play in the old wooden tennis-court, and sense the agelessness which derives from its position around the ancient citadel of the castle.

If the Moat Garden brings an air of natural charm to the centre of the castle, the formality of the East Terrace Garden continues to be in harmony with the regality of the buildings, as Wyatville originally intended. During the Second World War the fourteen flower-beds, which had been filled each year with two displays of spring and summer bedding plants, were planted with ingenious patterns of vegetables in response to the critical food shortage. After the war the beds were re-organized into a more simple pattern planned by the Duke of Edinburgh and filled with roses chosen by The Queen. The statue of Hercules and Acalus was replaced by the present tulip fountain in the centre of the circular pond. In 1976 the quantity of sculpture on the terrace was reduced when a number of the marble statues, some carved by Francavilla and brought there by George IV, and the two colossal vases by Edward Pearce and C. G. Cibber which he removed to the terrace from Hampton Court (described in that chapter), were presented to the nation and placed in the Orangery at Kensington Palace.

Despite these losses it is still the sculptures which dominate the East Terrace Garden to give it a look of Italian Renaissance gardens. Around the central parterre four bronze figures and lead vases on pedestals alternate with domed yews, their motionless features enhancing the simplicity of the pattern. They were cast for Charles I by Hubert le Sueur after classical figures, and represent the Borghese Gladiator, Hercules, Hermes and Artemis. During the reign of Charles II they stood at the end of the Long Water in St James's Park. They were removed to the Great Fountain Garden of Hampton Court by William III, from whence George IV brought them to Windsor. The four vases are by Willem van Mieris and represent the Seasons. They had originally stood in a garden in Leiden and were bought by George IV in 1825 from a Mr Graham to whom the King paid £472 10s. At the foot of the slope leading down from the north side of the garden to the Orangery is a lone recumbent figure in bronze by Lord Ronald Gower, the aristocratic son of the Duke of Sutherland, upon whom Oscar Wilde is said to have based Lord Henry Wotton in *The Portrait of Dorian Gray*. Dated 1876, it was cast by the Parisian founders Thiebaut & Fils and is romantically entitled 'La Garde Meurt et ne se rende pas'. The flights of steps from the sunken terrace on the east and south sides are surmounted by pairs of marble and lead vases; but of all the sculptures the supreme ornament is the bronze copy of the famous Warwick Vase, the same size as the original, which stands between the flights of steps leading down from the terrace below the east front of the castle. The white marble original was brought to Warwick Castle in 1774 by George Greville, Earl of Warwick, after its discovery in 1770 during excavations near Pantanello in Italy. It is probably the version mentioned by Puckler-Muskau in *The English Tour of Prince Puckler-Muskau described in his letters 1826–1828*, where he wrote, 'Among other things, I saw the copy of the Warwick Vase, of the same size as the original. It is cast in bronze, and cost four thousand pounds . . .' Around the vase are four lead water-butts carved with the monogram and crown of Charles II.

The East Terrace Garden arguably contains the finest collection of statuary of any of the Royal Gardens, and their various commissioning and provenances reflect the continuing tradition of Royal patronage. Arranged on the terrace they give the necessary elevation and quality of grandeur to the rather flat design of lawns and flowerbeds, and present a prospect which does not fail the architecture of the east front.

HAMPTON COURT

Middlesex

HAMPTON COURT was a manor of considerable size and importance before the famous period in its history began in 1514 with Cardinal Wolsey's tenure of the property. From the beginning of the fourteenth century it was owned by the Knights Hospitallers of St John of Jerusalem who at that time were at the height of their power and prosperity. The order owned property throughout England and the continent of Europe, and realized a considerable income from farming and rents. It is certain that the monastic and ecclesiastical orders were largely responsible for keeping alive the cultivation of gardens between the departure of the Romans and the Reformation, and it is recorded in Lyson's *Middlesex Parishes* that there was a garden at Hampton, as well as a manor-house, a 'camera' (or preceptory) and a dove-cote. This medieval garden was the first stage in four centuries of unbroken development and change in the gardens at Hampton Court, during which time they became a remarkable example of the evolution of English gardens.

By 1514 Wolsey was fast approaching the zenith of his power, in a position of unassailable supremacy next to that of the King, in affairs of Church and State. Hampton Court answered his need for a residence within reach of London, free from the city's unhealthy atmosphere and the danger of disease. After searching for a suitable site with characteristic thoroughness, on 11 January 1514 he leased the manor of Hampton Court for a term of ninety-nine years for £50 per annum, and his tenure began on 24 June – the day of the nativity of St John the Baptist. In many ways Cardinal Wolsey established what was to be Hampton Court's life even after he had left it. For he visualized a palace which would be without peer in England or Europe – a visible symbol of his wealth and power. And

Opposite : William III's Great Fountain Garden, now dominated by the enormous yews which hide all but the central pediment of Wren's east front

once built it was to be enjoyed, to have attention lavished upon it, to be a place of pleasure. As Hampton Court's history unfolded these motives for its conception constantly recurred, in its buildings and contents and equally in its parks and gardens.

At Hampton, where the land was half surrounded by the Thames' majestic curve, and the air was reported to contain an 'extraordinary salubrity', Wolsey indulged his architectural ambitions in the building and embellishing of a palace which was a masterpiece of Tudor architecture. It was not long before its parapets and gables, cupolas and clusters of wrought chimneys in red and purple brick formed the distinctive skyline.

Wolsey's private apartments were in the south front of his new palace, and it was below their windows that he laid out the gardens described here by George Cavendish:

> 'My gardens sweet enclosed with walles strong
> Embanked with benches to sit and take my rest
> The knotts so enknotted it cannot be exprest
> With arbours and alyes so pleasant and dulce
> The pestilent ayres with flavours to repulse.'

Knot gardens were to become a popular feature of Tudor landscape and were made up of intricate patterns of low hedges – of herbs such as box, lavender or rosemary – surrounding small beds of mixed flowers which were trained to the same height as the hedges. Wolsey's gardens extended from his Knot Garden to the site of the present Orangery Garden and Pond Garden. It is of that time, at the height of his popularity with the King, that we read of Wolsey walking with Henry VIII in the gardens at Hampton Court, the latter's arm around his shoulders in a manner of friendly confidence.

Hampton Court was the scene of many of the great diplomatic triumphs which played such a fundamental part in the achievements of Wolsey's career, and reflected most clearly the genius of his statesmanship. Cavendish reports in his *Life of Wolsey* that, 'All ambassadors of foreign potentates were always despatched by his directions. His house was always resorted to and furnished with noblemen, gentlemen, and other persons, with going and coming in and out, feasting and banquetting all ambassadors at divers times, and other strangers right nobly.' The impression which Wolsey himself made on his visitors can only have been enhanced by the grandeur of his surroundings at Hampton Court. Giustinian, the Venetian ambassador certainly felt so: 'All the power of the State is centred in him, he is, in fact, *ipse rex*, and no one in this realm dare attempt aught in opposition to his interests.'

It was the very loftiness of Wolsey's position that led to his downfall in the 1520s. He had numerous enemies who continually subjected him to satirical attacks. John Skelton, one of the most vociferous, wrote the poem 'Why Come Ye not to Court':

> 'Why come ye not to Court?
> To whyche Court?
> To the Kynges Court,
> Or to Hampton Court?
> Nay to the Kynges Court:
> But Hampton Court
> Hath the preemynence,
> And Yorkes Place,
> With my lorde's grace,
> To whose magnifycence
> Is all the conflewence,
> Sutys and supplycacyons
> Embassades of all nacyons . . .'

Wolsey knew that he was safe from these attacks as long as he enjoyed the King's favour, but even as his new palace neared completion his star was waning. In 1525 the King is reported to have asked Wolsey, with obvious jealousy, 'why he had built so magnificent a house for himself at Hampton Court'. Wolsey's deft reply, 'To show how noble a palace a subject may offer to his sovereign,' played into Henry VIII's scheming hands, for the King instantly took the offer literally and from that year the lease of Hampton Court, with all its fabulous possessions, passed to the King. Wolsey lived on at Hampton Court for four more years, in much the same style as he had previously enjoyed. But then came his final ruin at the King's hands. He was banished first to Esher Place, stripped of all power and possessions, and then to his diocese of York. It was while travelling as a prisoner of the King from York to London to attend his trial for high treason that Wolsey died, at Leicester Abbey on 29 November 1959 – a sadly unjust end for such a mighty statesman who did so much to strengthen the Tudors not only in England, but as a power to be reckoned with in Europe.

In his desire to alter and expand Hampton Court to even greater magnificence than Wolsey's, Henry VIII rivalled the Cardinal with extravagance. New buildings such as the Great Hall, galleries and apartments were being planned by him soon after Wolsey's death, as were extensive alterations to the grounds. It was not long before the King's arms and badges, lavishly painted and gilded, appeared adorning the brickwork throughout the palace – a visible sign of Royal ownership – and the roofscape became animated by a host of heraldic beasts, each clasping a vane guilded with a Tudor badge or part of the Royal arms, perhaps a rose, the fleur-de-lys or the crown.

The two parks which Wolsey had originally enclosed – Bushy Park and the House Park – comprising most of the two thousand acres of land

Overleaf: The Rose Garden on the site of Henry VIII's Tilt Yard. Beyond, his Great Hall – one of England's outstanding examples of Tudor architecture – rises to dominate the surviving parts of the Tudor palace

surrounding the palace, were quickly stocked with deer: hunting was one of the King's favourite pastimes. Indeed, one of the great attractions of Hampton Court for the King was his ability to indulge there in the various sporting activities he enjoyed so much, as well as hunting, shooting, hawking, fishing and jousting. For the purpose of the latter the area to the north of the palace was converted into a Tilt Yard where, with a glittering display of pomp, jousting took place with Henry VIII frequently taking part. One of the towers from which the spectators used to watch the competing knights survives beside the area still known as the Tilt Yard Garden. One of Henry VIII's earliest additions at Hampton Court was the Tennis Court, the oldest in England, where the King played regularly with great skill, as recorded by the ever-flattering Venetian ambassador, Giustinian, 'He is extremely fond of tennis, at which game it is the prettiest thing in the world to see him play, his fair skin glowing through a shirt of the finest texture.'

As well as surmounting the gables and parapets of the palace the King's heraldic beasts were to be found throughout his gardens, mounted on pedestals painted in the Tudor colours of green and white stripes. Many parts of the existing gardens were considerably altered and the total area was greatly expanded. Alongside the Pond Garden on the south front was laid out the 'King's New Garden', which led down to the Mount Garden beside the river. Here, on the raised ground called the Mount, the King built his Great Round Arbour where he could rest after arriving by barge from London. The path which wound up to the Arbour from the waterside was lined by heraldic beasts standing like sentinels with their boldly emblazoned vanes. The Mount was surrounded by a low hedge of rosemary which, like many herbs, was of great importance in Tudor gardens; it was very popular with the then Lord Chancellor, Sir Thomas More, in his gardens in Chelsea.

These gardens to the south of the palace, as well as their ponds, herb hedges and heraldic beasts, were filled with traditional English flowers – violets, roses, gillyflowers and hyacinths – and were for the King's pleasure. In the eighteen years between 1529 and Henry VIII's death in 1547 all six of his wives spent some time at Hampton Court; but it is perhaps with Anne Boleyn, Jane Seymour or Catherine Howard that he is most likely to have passed the hours wandering lovesick in his gardens. How ironic it is that so many of the dramatic events at the end of their three lives took place there. After the turbulent months of her love-affair with the King, and his divorce from Catherine of Aragon, Anne Boleyn spent many of the happiest hours of her triumphant three years as Queen at Hampton Court; and we know that she was fond of sitting occupied with her needlework on the path raised beside the King's New Garden and sheltered by a bower of hornbeam. But it was most probably in a room at Hampton Court that she discovered Jane Seymour meekly sitting on the King's knee, submitting to his intimate caresses. Anne's indignant anger

and subsequent miscarriage of a boy led to the King's final determination to be rid of her. It was only a year later, in 1537, that Jane Seymour, of whom Henry VIII had grown particularly fond, died at Hampton Court two weeks after giving birth to the King's only son. And in 1541 the legend was born of a gallery haunted by the screaming ghost of Catherine Howard. The King and his new Queen were at Hampton Court when Cranmer revealed to Henry evidence, prepared by Catherine's enemies, of indiscretions before her marriage. Catherine was confined to her rooms, but at one time escaped to attempt to plead her case with the King. It was after his refusal to see her that she is reported to have run, screaming his name, along the gallery behind the Chapel, but to no avail. The King departed from Hampton the next day, and shortly afterwards Catherine was removed to Sion House before her execution on Tower Hill.

As well as the gardens to the south of the palace Henry VIII laid out two orchards next to the Tilt Yard. These orchards would not have been filled exclusively with fruit trees, as the word in its modern sense suggests, but with a variety of trees; they were reported to have contained cypress, yew and bay trees removed from the monastic gardens at Sion, Richmond and Charterhouse, filling the area later to be called the Wilderness.

Henry VIII's life at Hampton Court contained many of the elements so characteristic of his reign – the splendour and pageantry, wealth and extravagance, the sport and relaxation of court life and, as well as the enjoyment, the dramas and rages which manifested themselves so frequently. By the time of his death the palace had become a triumphant monument to the Tudors but the atmosphere had become very different from that which Wolsey had established.

After the brief interlude of the reigns of Edward VI and Mary, the Tudor dynasty, and Hampton Court with it, was restored to its former glory during the reign of Elizabeth I. Elizabeth was very fond of her father's great palace and visited it regularly, happy to enjoy the buildings as they were without altering or enlarging them. She also took great interest in the gardens and, as well as ensuring that they were well maintained, made a number of alterations. No doubt William Cecil had some influence on the changing contents of the flower and herb gardens, for his gardens at Cecil House in the Strand, and at Theobalds Park, were widely renowned. Cecil was constantly receiving plants from his envoys abroad, such as the Turk's-cap lily from Turkey, some of which possibly found their way to Hampton Court. And other strange plants from abroad began to appear, delivered to the Queen by her discoverers Drake, Hawkyns and Raleigh. Visitors to Hampton Court never failed to be impressed by the gardens, as Hentnzer shows in his *Travels in England* where he records that the gardens were noted for the: 'sundry towers, or rather bowers for places of recreation and solace, and for sundry other uses;' and for: 'the rosemary so nailed and planted to the walls as to cover them entirely, which is a manner exceeding common in England, and laid out with various other plants, which are trained, intertwined and trimmed in so wonderful a manner, and in such extraordinary shapes, that the like could not easily be found'.

Perhaps the best impression of Tudor gardens, such as those at Hampton Court, is given by Francis Bacon in his *Essay on Gardens*. Bacon argues that a garden should contain things of beauty for the different times of the year: for the winter, evergreen trees and herbs such as holly, juniper yew, rosemary and lavender; later in spring, early flowers like primroses, anemones, violets and daffodils, and fruit blossom; in summer, a great variety of flowers including wallflowers, lilies, gillyflowers, roses and lilac trees; and in the autumn, a predominance of fruit – pears, plums, apples and apricots. Another account showing the reputation of Hampton Court's gardens is Harrison's *Description of England*. 'If you look into our gardens annexed to our houses, how wonderfullie is their beauty increased, not onelie with floures and varieties of curious and costlie workmanship, but also with rare and medicinal hearbes sought up in the land within these fortie years.' After discussing his own garden Harrison concludes, 'If therefore my little plot, void of all art in keeping be so well furnished, what shall we think of those at Hampton Court, Nonesuch etc?'

Hampton Court's distance from London and Elizabeth's habit of retiring there for rest and quiet often encouraged her to use it for meetings and interviews which she desired to keep secret or private. One of the great issues of Elizabeth's reign was the question of whom she was to marry; and it was in the Privy Garden at Hampton Court in 1559 that the Queen met the first in a long series of suitors, the Earl of Arran. The meeting was surrounded by the greatest secrecy because Arran, the Protestant son of the Duc de Châtelherault was heir to the Scottish throne if Mary Queen of Scots died childless. News of this possible union with the English Queen had therefore to be kept from the Scots. As events turned out Arran was as unsuccessful as those who followed him, for Elizabeth left the interview determined not to marry him.

The suitors came and went, the Queen remained unmarried; but it was again at Hampton Court in 1561 that the scandalous rumour of Elizabeth's affair with her favourite, Lord Robert Dudley, became widespread, fired by the story that the Queen had given birth there to a son fathered by him. The gossip only abated when Elizabeth became critically ill with smallpox, and attention was diverted by this far more dangerous matter. Dudley, who became the Earl of Leicester, continued as the Queen's favourite. Some years later Sir James Melville who, as Mary Queen of Scots' agent, frequently visited Hampton Court, recorded how Elizabeth on one occasion showed him a miniature of Dudley which she kept with others in a cabinet in her bedchamber; on the paper which wrapped the picture was written, 'My Lord's Picture'. On another occasion when Elizabeth had made an appointment to meet Melville in the

gardens at eight o'clock in the morning, he noted that the Queen regularly walked in the gardens at that hour, usually briskly, 'to catch her a heate in the colde mornings'; but when she was accompanied, 'she who was the very image of majesty and magnificence, went slowly and marched with leisure.'

Henry VIII had built the Cloister Green Court on the site of Wolsey's Knot Garden, but during Elizabeth I's reign, when this form of garden enjoyed a peak of popularity, she revived the Knot Garden below the south front, where there is a stone with her monogram and the date 1568. The brightly coloured and highly complex designs appealed to the Elizabethan mind, and interest was further attracted by the publication of a book in 1577 by Didymus Mountaine called *Gardener's Labyrinth*. In it Mountaine writes that a Knot Garden should, 'give such grace to the garden, that the place will seem like a tapestry of flowers'.

Opposite: The Tudor Knot Garden, reconstructed in 1924 by Ernest Law, stands on the site of the sixteenth-century original

The small-scale formality of the seventeenth-century Pond Garden and William III's Banqueting House contrasts with the overpowering size of the main palace and grounds.

The death of Elizabeth marked the end of the florid Tudor era of which Hampton Court remains so reminiscent. Nowhere captured more completely the character of the dynasty and their bold Renaissance advance from the medieval world which still dominated England at the end of the fifteenth century. During the reign of James I there was little change at Hampton Court and the King enjoyed it mainly for stag-hunting in the parks, which he re-stocked with a prodigious number of deer. His wife, Queen Anne, delighted in the performance of masques, which became so fashionable at court during his reign. Before their first Christmas as King and Queen there were great preparations for such a masque at Hampton Court, which included rifling through Queen Elizabeth's wardrobe, and making use of numerous of her huge selection of dresses as costumes.

During Charles I's reign the first signs of new styles in gardens began to appear at Hampton Court. They originated in the gardens of Italian Renaissance villas, filled with pergolas, loggias, elaborate fountains and waterworks, and statuary. Many of these features were not suited to England because of the need for steep slopes; but at Hampton Court the circular pond in the centre of the Privy Garden was transformed by the addition of a black marble fountain surmounted by a 'brasse' (bronze) figure by Francesco Fanelli, a one-eyed sculptor who was paid an annuity by the King. The fountain contained scrolls, sea-monsters, sirens and boys holding dolphins, all spouting water, and the figure was most likely to have been Venus as she holds a golden apple (though in the Commonwealth Inventory of 1653 she was referred to as Arethusa and later, also mistakenly, as Diana). Fanelli also made bronze statues of Venus and Cleopatra and white marble ones of Adonis and Apollo, which stood in the Privy Garden. These statues were the first to replace the heraldic lions, leopards, harts and antelopes which, with their glittering vanes, were so distinctively Tudor.

Charles I was a man of impeccable artistic taste who during his lifetime built up a unique collection of works of art. Hampton Court was filled with many of these: of the almost countless paintings in the palace he was reputed to have bought four hundred – including the nine pictures by Andrea Mantegna of 'The Triumph of Caesar', painted between 1485 and 1492, which are among his greatest work. Much of the collection disappeared from Hampton Court and elsewhere during the years of the Commonwealth or afterwards, but happily a great part has remained. As well as his addition of the Fanelli fountain and statues, Charles I's interest in gardens is shown by the fact that he employed John Tradescant II who, with his father and son, was one of a famous Dutch gardening trio. Tradescant reputedly introduced the Tulip Tree into England. The King also employed John Parkinson, who held the post of Botanicus Regius Primarius and in 1629 published *Paradisi in Sole, Paradisus Terrestus,* acknowledged as a major contribution to English garden literature.

Left : One of the pair of lead statues of Venus and Cleopatra, returned to the Privy Garden in 1933, which stand looking along the overhung paths of the garden. Plants such as the red and white peonies add colour beneath the foliage of the trees

Above : The statue of Spring in the Privy Garden. Cast by Robert Jackson in 1869, it maintains the tradition of beautiful statues which have adorned the Hampton Court Gardens

During the Civil War and Commonwealth Hampton Court narrowly averted being sold off by Parliament. However, such a bastion of the monarchy was unlikely to escape unscathed, and considerable damage was wrought by the Puritans in the chapel: the pulling down of 'popish and superstitious pictures'. A comprehensive inventory of the palace was drawn up with a view to sale, but eventually it was decided to retain it and most of its contents for the Commonwealth; and Hampton later became the residence of Oliver Cromwell during his Protectorate.

The restoration of Charles II heralded the renewal of those sojourns by King and court which were Hampton's lifeblood. It also saw the start of changes which, when continued so dramatically by William and Mary, were to transform the Tudor palace into part of the French-orientated world of the late seventeenth century. Charles had spent most of his exile in France and must have been aware of the radical changes that were taking place in garden design. The intimate enclosed gardens of medieval (and Tudor) times were being swept away and replaced with lay-outs of vast formality. Charles would have seen the new gardens of the Tuileries, where one of the gardeners who influenced the designs was le Nôtre – father of André le Nôtre. More importantly, he certainly saw André le Nôtre's early work at Vaux-le-Vicomte, the chateau of Louis XIV's Chancellor Fouquet. Le Nôtre was quickly taken on by Louis XIV, to help with the laying out of the gardens at Versailles, where his designs were to elevate even the grandeur of that huge palace.

On his restoration Charles II wasted no time in writing to ask Louis XIV if le Nôtre could come to England. Louis agreed but there is no record that le Nôtre ever did come. However, Charles was undeterred; although le Nôtre may have influenced and given advice on the design at Hampton Court, the work was supervised by John Rose, who had previously been sent by the Earl of Essex to study under le Nôtre and was arguably the founder of the Anglo-French school of gardening. (Rose was also famous for successfully growing the first pineapple in England, and is immortalized in the painting by Thomas Danckerts, which shows Rose presenting the fruit to Charles II in front of Ham House.) The new ideas were put into practise on the east front of Hampton Court which looked out on to the flat expanse of the park. Three lime avenues were planted, radiating in a semi-circular *patte d'oie* or 'goose foot', stretching away into the park as far as the eye could see. An idea of their size is to be found in the King's order to a certain Christian van Vranen for four thousand trees to be brought from Holland. A wide canal was dug, extending its whole length down the main central avenue, which led away from the centre of the east front. By 1662 John Evelyn, the diarist and renowned horticulturalist, was able to write that, 'The Park, formerly a naked piece of ground, (*is*) now planted with sweet rows of lime trees; and the canal for water near perfected.' And one feels that Sir George Sitwell may well have been thinking of Hampton Court when he wrote in his essay *On the*

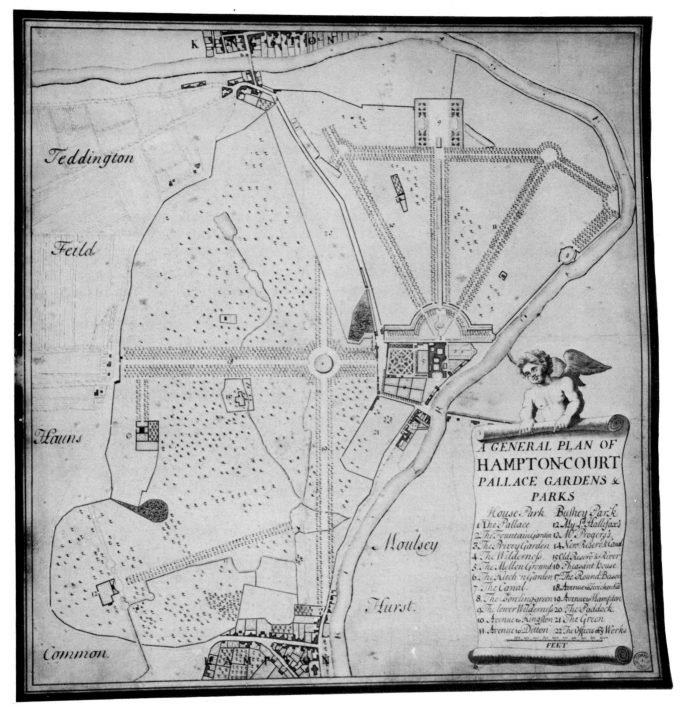

A GENERAL PLAN OF
HAMPTON-COURT
PALLACE GARDENS &
PARKS

House Park.   Bushey Park.
1 The Pallace   12 My Lr Hallifax's
2 The Fountain Garden   13 Mr Progers's
3 The Privey Garden   14 New Reserv. Land
4 The Wildernefs   15 Old Reserv. & River
5 The Mellon Ground   16 Pheasant House
6 The Kitchen Garden   17 The Round Bason
7 The Canal   18 Avenue Teddington
8 The Bowling-green   19 Avenue Hampton
9 The lower Wildernefs 20 The Paddock
10 Avenue to Kingston   21 The Green
11 Avenue to Ditton   22 The Offices & Works

FEET

Making of Gardens, a passage discussing the use of water: 'The grandest effect of all is produced by formal canals, not too large, which reflect the pavilion in the far end and the lime avenues which hedge them in.' The development of Charles II's gardens at Hampton Court was closely connected with similar work at Greenwich and St James's Park. It is very likely that two other great French gardeners – Gabriel and André Mollet – were associated with the work in all three gardens. André Mollet's book

Bridgeman's eighteenth-century plan of Hampton Court, showing Charles II's *patte d'oie* and the later avenues of Bushy Park

Le Jardin de Plaisir, was dedicated to Charles II and in it Mollet suggests that in a *patte d'oie* the avenues should radiate from a semi-circle of trees, as is the case in all three of Charles II's gardens.

The coming and goings of Charles II's court were constantly remarked upon by John Evelyn and, of course, the other great diarist of the time, Samuel Pepys. As well as noting the new improvements to the east front, Evelyn passed his critical eye over the gardens on the south front of the palace and concluded: 'In the garden is a rich and noble fountain, with syrens, statues, etc, cast in copper by Fanelli, but no plenty of water. The cradle walk of horn-beam in the garden is, for the perplexed twining of the trees, very observable. There is a parterre which they call Paradise, in which is a pretty banqueting house set over a cave or cellar. All these gardens might be exceedingly improved, as being too narrow for such a palace.'

As his predecessors had done so often, Charles II used Hampton Court for the entertainment of foreign guests, diplomats and envoys. The cross-section of impressions which they retained shows not only how rarely they failed to be impressed but also gives a rich variety of comment which, by virtue of the immediacy with which it was committed to paper, brings alive the palace of two centuries ago. In 1669 one distinguished visitor was Cosmo III, Duke of Tuscany, whose secretary, Magalotti, wrote *Travels of Cosmo III in England*. Extolling the virtues of Hampton Court he says: 'The gardens are divided into very large, level and well kept walks which, separating the ground into different compartments, form artificial pastures of grass, being themselves formed by espalier trees, partly such as bear fruit, and partly ornamental ones, but all adding to the beauty of the appearance. This beauty is further augmented by the fountains made of slate after the Italian style, and distributed in different parts of the garden, whose *jets d'eaux* throw up the water in various playful and fanciful ways. There are also in the gardens some snug places of retirement in certain towers, formerly intended as places of accommodation for the King's mistresses.' Magalotti's mention of the 'artificial pastures of grass' is particularly interesting – it was during the Stuart period that lawns of cut grass took the place of stretches of camomile or wild grass, uncut and sprinkled with flowers.

Although Charles II was to some extent hampered in his plans for Hampton Court by a lack of space and money, his transformation of the east front and the park was the basis of their appearance today. It is doubtful whether his brother, James II, ever stayed at Hampton Court during his short reign; and the 'Glorious Revolution' of 1688, when he lost the throne to his daughter Mary and nephew and son-in-law, William of Orange, was the most important watershed in Hampton Court's history. William's lack of sympathy with many English customs was shown in different ways. One was his abhorrence of the tradition for the monarch to eat in public when at the old palace of Whitehall, and another his opinion of the old superstition of 'touching for the King's evil' – in 1689 he rewarded the scrofulous petitioners who arrived at Hampton Court with the words: 'It is a silly superstition, give the poor creatures some money and let them go.' This disinterest was undoubtedly influential in his decision to demolish the unrivalled architectural legacy of the Tudor monarchs.

In *London Fabric* James Pope-Hennessy gave his verdict on the changes which William and Mary made at Hampton Court. 'From an interesting monument of the English Renaissance, Hampton Court was

Wren's spectacular Fountain Court which replaced Henry VIII's Cloister Green Court. Against the skyline are the patterned outlines of some of the surviving Tudor chimneys

transformed into a Dutch copy of Versailles.' During his first visit to Hampton Court shortly after his arrival in England, it was clear that William delighted in the palace's riverside situation, in its distance from London – for which he had no affection – and in the flatness of the surrounding countryside; and he determined to spend a great deal of his time there. The only thing that did not appeal to him was the palace itself, with its irregular buildings and lack of 'modern conveniences'. He proposed to overcome the problem by demolishing most of the old Tudor palace and erecting a new building, which by its style and grandeur would rival – and even possibly excel – Louis XIV's great palace at Versailles.

Sir Christopher Wren was the architect entrusted with William's ambitions, and it was not long before the buildings around Henry VIII's Cloister Green Court crumbled to the ground to be replaced by a new quadrangle named the Fountain Court, of which the south and east sides formed the imposing new south and east fronts. Wren's task was not easy because as well as aiming to blend his new edifice with the existing buildings he had constantly to accommodate William's personal desires. What we see today of Wren's alterations to Hampton Court are only part of William's complete plan which, if carried out would have resulted in the demolition of even more of the old Tudor palace. The King's apartments were to be along the south front and the Queen's along the east. To compliment these new apartments a grand entrance court three hundred yards wide with adjoining rooms was planned for the north of the palace.

While the building was in progress William and Mary turned their attention to the gardens which would complement the regular brickwork, stone-dressed windows and columns of Wren's massive façades. George London, who had been a pupil of John Rose and who took over his position as head gardener at Hampton Court, supervised the work assisted by his partner, Henry Wise, although it appears that much of the design was the result of ideas which came from William and Mary themselves. Stephen Switzer, a noted horticulturalist who at one time worked under London and Wise showed a keen interest in the developments at Hampton Court, and reported that, 'It is certain the Prince did plant the large semi-circle before the palace at Hampton Court in pursuance of some great Design in Gard'ning. The foundation of great designs being thus laid out by their Royal Uncle, it was thought to be one great inducement to those Princes [William and Mary] to take up their chief residence there, and Gard'ning soon felt the happy effect of it. The great garden, the garden next the river, call'd now the Privay Garden; and the Wilderness and Kitchen Gardens [both on the north] were made with great dispatch. The only fault was the pleasure gardens being stuff'd too thick with box, a fashion brought over out of Holland by the Dutch gardeners, who us'd it to a fault, especially in England where we abound in so good grass and gravel. But upon all other accounts the gardens were noble and their Majesties' designs yet nobler ...'

The seemingly endless vista of the Great Broad Walk, laid out by London and Wise for William III, stretches beyond the east front of the palace. Wren's elegant façade looks out on to the yews of the Great Fountain Garden, where Charles II's three avenues converge

As Switzer points out, Charles II's semi-circular arch of lime trees, which linked the ends of the three main avenues, left a dome-shaped space before the east front and there William laid out a parterre called the Great Fountain Garden. The plans necessitated filling in 200 yards of the canal so that it began at the top of the semi-circle. In the centre of the parterre was a large fountain with others spaced around it. Between the fountains were patterns of box scrollwork divided by yew trees, clipped into pyramids, alternating with circular holly trees. The outstanding ornaments of this garden were the two vases flanking its entrance from the palace. One, by Gabriel Cibber, a Dane who did extensive carving work for the new buildings, was described as, 'a great Vauze of white marble, enricht with divers ornaments, with a pedestal of Portland stone, also enricht'. The other, made by Edward Pearce, was similarly described. It was obviously these two vases which Daniel Defoe mentioned in 1724 when writing about Hampton Court: 'At the entrance gate into the garden stand advanced, on two pedestals of stone, two marble Vases or Flower-Pots of most exquisite workmanship, the one done by an Englishman, the other by a German.'

During the early years of his reign William was frequently away from England, in Ireland or on the continent – often in his native Holland. Mary, who shared his affection for and interest in Hampton Court, spent as much time as possible there, away from London; and while the new apartments were being built she took up residence in the old Water Gallery that had been occupied by Queen Elizabeth during the reign of Mary Tudor. The interior was redecorated under Wren's supervision and amongst the panels, cornices and painted ceilings was some of Grinling Gibbons' beautiful carving, a notable addition to the new state apartments.

While at Hampton Court Mary occupied most of her time in 'the innocent diversions of building and Gardenage'. Unlike her husband, whose principal horticultural interest was grandiose designs and garden ornament, Mary was keenly interested in botany and, encouraged by her trusted herbalist, Dr Plunkenet, the limits of her quests for rare and exotic plants knew no bounds. The records in one instance reveal the cost of a trip to Virginia: 'For going to Virginia to make a collection of foreign plants – £234 11s 9d.' One specimen brought to Hampton Court was the *Agave americana variegata*, whose common name, the 'Century Plant', derives from its reputation to take a hundred years to flower. The plant brought to Hampton Court did succeed in flowering but exceeded even legend, for its first blooms appeared two hundred years after its arrival.

To accommodate those plants which demanded warmth during the winter a number of hothouses were erected – in the old Privy Garden, along the south side of the palace, beside Wolsey's old apartments; and opposite the Pond Garden Wren built a long Orangery. Other new additions were orange trees – with their obvious political connotations – and lemon trees, many of which came from William's garden at Loo. After

Mary's death William altered the old Pond Garden into small enclosures surrounded by protective hedges, where 'exotick' plants could be kept during the summer.

William and Mary's activities in the gardens brought in many fashions popular in Holland which, although they retained their French names, contrasted with the spacious grandeur of the French style of le Nôtre. One such fashion was for *treillage*, or trellis work, of which Hampton Court contains a notable example in Queen Mary's Bower (renamed from the days of Anne Boleyn). A long avenue of wych elms completely covered in by a roof of intertwined branches, it stretched along the terrace between the Privy and Pond Gardens right down to the river. Here Queen Mary took great delight in sitting and sewing with her ladies and since her death the terrace has always been known as Queen Mary's Bower. The likeness of many of Queen Mary's attendants was preserved for posterity by Kneller in his series of portraits known as the 'Hampton Court Beauties'. These were painted for the Queen in an attempt to rival Lely's wonderful series, commissioned by the Duchess of York, the 'Beauties of the Court of Charles II'; but the latter's intriguing sensuality gives them a charm which Kneller's uniform series never attained.

Another Dutch fashion was for *clairvoyées*, ornamental iron grills between pillars, the view through which gave the sensation of a larger landscape beyond, and Hampton Court possesses one of the supreme examples in Europe of this device. William and Mary employed Jean Tijou, the unrivalled French designer of wrought iron work, to provide a variety of his exquisite designs for Hampton Court; these include the balustrade for the King's new staircase inside the palace, the gates which lead from the east front into the gardens, and other gates throughout the grounds. But his greatest contribution was the unique screen of twelve panels, each over 10 feet high and 13 feet wide, which stands on the riverside at the south end of the Privy Garden. An unrivalled masterpiece, the intricate scrollwork of each panel contains a small central panel with such designs as a harp, thistle, rose or the Garter. During the nineteenth century the screens were removed to the Victoria and Albert Museum, but in 1902 they were returned to their rightful present position. It is a sad picture of injustice which reveals Tijou still petitioning Queen Anne in 1703 for £1889 1s 6¼d – nearly the total of the bill for his work at Hampton Court – and that he still did not receive payment until twelve years after the work was completed. The craftsman who executed the delicate foliated scroll-work of Tijou's designs was an Englishman, Huntingdon Shaw, and Tijou's work was undoubtedly the inspiration for men whose work appeared in many English gardens in the eighteenth century, such as Robert Bakewell, one of his pupils.

Much had been achieved at Hampton Court, but much still remained to do when, in 1694, Queen Mary died without ever occupying her new state apartments. This tragic loss drove William away from Hampton, so full of memories of his Queen, as Switzer records in his *Ichnographia Rustica*: 'Upon the death of that illustrious Princess, gardening and all other pleasures were under an eclipse with that Prince; and the beloved Hampton Court for some time lay unregarded.' It was not until 1698, when the ancient home of English monarchy, Whitehall Palace, was destroyed by fire, that William's interest in Hampton was revived. He candidly revealed his true opinion of Whitehall's loss in his secret correspondence with his friend Heinsius: 'The loss is less to me than it would be to another person, for I cannot live there.'

On William's return to Hampton Court there is evidence that while his new apartments were being completed plans for a new north entrance were being drawn up. The first, and only, stage to be completed was the laying-out of Bushy Park in its present form. The road cut across the park, broken only by the enormous Basin later to hold the Diana Fountain, ran between four avenues of limes and, closest to it, an avenue of chestnuts – in all 732 lime trees and 274 chestnuts; joining the Basin at right-angles were two shorter avenues. The Wilderness, between Bushy Park and the palace to the north, was laid out by London and Wise at about the same time. Something as far removed from the modern idea of a wilderness would be harder to imagine, for the area was filled with a series of geometrically designed paths surrounded by clipped hedges and trees of holly, yew and box. In the centre was a complex circular pattern of espalier trees called Troy Town.

Many of the trees in the Wilderness were transplanted by Wise from the Privy Garden. William had ordered that the Privy Garden be lowered in order to afford better views of the river from his new apartments. At the same time the riverside prospect was further cleared by the levelling of Henry VIII's Mount and the destruction of the Water Gallery – a loss to some extent recompensed by the appearance of the Banqueting House, a small castellated lodge beside the new Great Terrace along the Thames, whence many of the carvings by Grinling Gibbons, saved from the Water Gallery, were removed.

William's main ambitions in the gardens had always focused on the east front – his Great Fountain Garden – and during the second phase of activity at Hampton Court he once again turned his attention to this semi-circular parterre. The number of fountains was increased to total thirteen and as Defoe remarked, no detail escaped William's attention: 'particularly the dimensions of the fountains, and what quantity of water they should cast up ...' As well as these improvements a far more ambitious transformation was made to the east front – the addition of the Great Broad Walk, the wide terrace which extends for 2,300 feet from the Kingston road straight across the front of the palace to the river where the Water Gallery had stood. The creation of the terrace necessitated the removal of the limes closest to the palace in the original semi-circle, and the extension of the parterre into two rectangular wings flanked on their

eastern (palace-facing) sides by avenues and a small canal. At the Kingston road entrance to the terrace the Flower-Pot Gates were erected, with piers of Portland stone surmounted by figures of boys carrying urns laden with flowers. These lead figures were moulded by Jan van Nost, the Dutch master-craftsman whose workshops were in London.

The death of William in 1702 brought to an end the continuous activity and revolutionary change which Hampton Court experienced throughout his reign. His fatal riding accident in the Park there, reputed to have been caused by a molehill, gave rise to the story of 'the little gentleman in black velvet' thereafter toasted by the Jacobites. However much we may agree with James Pope-Hennessy in deploring the destruction of so much of the old Tudor building and with it the loss of Tudor atmosphere at Hampton, it cannot be denied that the scale of William and Mary's work was remarkable and their efforts determined the present appearance of both palace and gardens.

'Close by these meads, for ever crowned with flowers,
Where Thames with pride surveys his rising towers,
There stands a structure of majestic frame,
Which from the neighb'ring Hampton takes its name.
Here Britain's statesmen oft the fall foredoom
Of foreign tyrants, and of nymphs at home;
Here thou, great *Anna*! whom three realms obey,
Dost sometimes councel take – and sometimes tea.'

Thus Alexander Pope, in *The Rape of the Lock*, described the palace during Queen Anne's reign. Anne was fond of Hampton Court and one of her main delights there was stag-hunting. On account of her grossness and immobility from gout and dropsy, she devised a novel mode of pursuit – by horse-drawn chaise. If we are to believe Jonathan Swift, her driving was fairly reckless, for he gives an account of his *Journal to Stella*: 'She hunts in a chaise with one horse, which she drives herself, and drives furiously like Jehu, and is a mighty hunter like Nimrod.'

Anne made a number of alterations to the gardens, but no major innovations. In the Great Fountain Garden she removed most of the clipped box from the parterre because of her intense dislike of its smell; and also the eight fountains which had formed the outer circle of William's design. This latter was done despite the ingenious proposals of Captain Thomas Savory, whose plans for improving the water-supply to the fountains by the use of a steam pump, were rejected. On the north edge of the Wilderness the huge stone piers of the Lion Gates bearing Anne's cypher were put up, but the gates between them did not appear until George I's reign; and despite being an example of the beautiful style of Tijou's work they nevertheless appear incongrously small and were originally intended for another part of the gardens. Next to the Lion Gates the famous Maze was constructed, whose winding paths extend to half a mile. It is this which seems to be referred to in a contemporary account of Hampton Court, which describes: 'a figure hedge-work, of very large evergreen plants in the Wilderness, to face the iron gates that are to be placed to take the middle line of the great avenue that runs through Bushy Park'.

One loss that the gardens sustained during Anne's reign was the removal of Fanelli's fountain from the Privy Garden to the Basin in Bushy Park. In 1712 Wren was instructed to supervise the re-casting of its figures and its removal to the new site. Marooned at a distance in the middle of the water with Venus (or Arethusa, or Diana as she was variously known) perched unappreciably high on the stonework, the whole creation loses its impact.

Shortly after his arrival from Hanover George I found Hampton Court one of the few agreeable features of his new kingdom whose people he disliked and could not understand, sentiments which were quite as heartily reciprocated. Away from the overpowering foreign atmosphere of London he could feel at home, surrounded by the Germanic entourage that included his two mistresses – Madame Schulenburg, who became Duchess of Kendal, and Madame Kilmansegge, who became Countess of Darlington and Leinster. These females' respective derisive titles, 'Maypole' and 'Elephant and Castle', reflect the contrasting nature of their figures which the King (and apparently no other) found so enticing. The two 'frows' were hardly likely to escape comment in an age of such widespread satire and public wit, and Horace Walpole gives in his *Reminiscences* a terrifying account of being introduced when a child to the 'Elephant and Castle':

'Her enormous figure was as corpulent and ample as the Duchess of Kendal's was long and emaciated. Two fierce ·black eyes, large and rolling, beneath two lofty arched eyebrows; two acres of cheek spread with crimson; an ocean of neck, that overflowed and was not distinguished from the lower part of her body, and no part restrained by stays: no wonder that a child dreaded such an ogress.'

In a letter written in 1717 to Teresa and Martha Blunt Pope describes the tedium of court life under George I:

'I went by water to Hampton Court, unattended by all but my own virtues, which were not of so modest a nature as to keep themselves, or me, concealed; for I met the Prince with all his ladies, on horseback, coming in from hunting. Mrs B[Bellenden] and Mrs L[Lepell] took me into protection, contrary to the laws against harbouring papists, and gave me a dinner, with something I like better, an opportunity of conversing with Mrs H[Howard]. We all agreed that the life of a Maid of Honour was of all things the most miserable: and wished that every woman who envied it had a specimen of it. To eat Westphalia ham in the morning, ride over hedges and ditches on borrowed hacks, come home in the heat of the day with a fever, and (what is worse a hundred times) with a red mark on the forehead from an uneasy hat! All this may qualify them to make excellent wives for foxhunters and bear abundance of ruddy complexioned children. As soon as they can wipe off the sweat of the day, they must simper an hour and catch cold in the Princess's apartment; from thence (as Shakespeare has it) to dinner, with what appetite they may; – and after that, till midnight, walk, work, or think, which they please. I can easily believe no lone house in Wales, with a mountain and a rookery, is more contemplative than this Court; and as a proof of it, I need only tell you Miss L[Lepell] walked with me three or four hours by moonlight, and we met no creature of any quality but the King, who gave audience to the Vice-Chamberlain, all alone, under the garden walk.

In short, I heard of no ball, assembly, basset table, or any place, where two or three were gathered together, except Madame Killmansegge's, to which I had the honour to be invited, and the grace to stay away.'

One period of light relief was provided for Hampton Court in the

Overleaf: Tijou's exquisite gates open onto one of the lime avenues forming the great *patte d'oie*. Four thousand trees were ordered from Holland by Charles II to fulfil his grand design

summer of 1716 when the Prince of Wales, who had recently been appointed Regent, resided at the palace with his wife and court in an atmosphere reminiscent of the days of the Restoration. The Prince and Princess were determined to show by the gaiety and brilliance of their court a marked contrast to that of George I, and during this stay they were certainly successful. The bowling-green which stood between Wren's four pavilions at the end of the Terrace Walk was a favourite spot during the evenings – as Dryden records:

> 'Hither in summer evenings you repair
> To taste the *fraicheur* of the cooler air.'

The atmosphere was full of 'frizelation' and 'dangleation' – the flirting and coquettish conversation which abounded. The two undisputed favourites of the court were Mary Bellenden and Molly Lepell; the former was pursued unceasingly by the Prince but to no avail, and both were constantly mentioned by the poets of the day, including Pope:

> 'What pranks are played behind the scenes,
> And who at court the belle;
> Some swear it is the Bellenden,
> And others say Lepell.'

1716 was the last year that Hampton Court was to enjoy a visit by so brilliant and amusing a court, and when the Prince of Wales ascended to the throne in 1727 the court settled down to a more sedate style. Among Queen Caroline's interests was gardening, and she was a keen disciple of the new 'landscape' school of which William Kent, who had been employed to redecorate parts of the interior of the palace, was a leading advocate. It was under his influence that she removed the scroll-work and fountains, save only the main central one, from the Great Fountain Garden and replaced them with lawns. It was Queen Caroline who first put flower-beds beneath the walls dividing the Broad Walk from, on one side the Privy Garden and on the other, the Wilderness. Since early Victorian times these borders have been steadily added to and expanded, to form the deep herbaceous borders of today.

The death of Queen Caroline in 1737 led to the virtual desertion of Hampton Court by George II and his court. His death in 1760 completed the break, for his grandson, George III, never lived there. The Duke of Sussex (a younger son of George III) argued that the reason for this stemmed from the occasion when George II was reported to have lost his temper with his grandson in one of the State apartments, and boxed his ears, leaving him with such unpleasant memories of Hampton that he had no desire to live there. George III's decision to cast off the palace as a residence made it virtually impossible for any of his successors to re-occupy it, had they so wished, for by the end of his sixty-year reign, most of the contents had been removed.

Although the palace was abandoned it was not allowed to fall into

disrepair. The care of the gardens during George III's reign was entrusted to Lancelot ('Capability') Brown, whose work the King admired. We can be thankful that when the King suggested to Brown he 'improve' the gardens in the modern style, Brown surprisingly declined, 'out of respect to himself and his profession'. One of the few alterations he did make, though, was to replace the flights of steps in the Privy Garden with grass terraces, arguing that, 'we ought not to go up and down stairs in the open air'.

It was also during George III's reign that one of the most famous additions was made to the gardens of Hampton Court – in 1768 the Great Vine was planted. The vine is one of the Black Hamburg variety, and came as a cutting from Valentine House near Ilford in Essex. The prolific growth of the vine has been limited only by the size of the glasshouse along whose walls it is trained.

During the late eighteenth century many of the rooms of the palace were occupied as apartments by people with a warrant from the Lord Chamberlain. This practice has continued ever since, and today the apartments are let as 'grace and favour' residences. Thus the palace was not left empty for too long; and during the reign of George IV the Royal presence was maintained to a degree as the Duke of Clarence, later William IV, was Ranger of Bushy Park and lived at Bushy House. George IV contributed to the disappearance of features in William III's Great Fountain Garden when he removed four statues and the two great vases by Cibber and Pearce, and took them to Windsor.

Shortly after her accession Queen Victoria decided in 1838 to open the State apartments and grounds of Hampton Court to the public, free of charge. The idea succeeded, and in 1839 115,971 people visited the palace. Though no longer occupied as a Royal residence, Hampton Court owes its continuing popularity to the fact that it is preserved as such.

In 1924 Ernest Law, who wrote three volumes on the *History of Hampton Court Palace*, and *Hampton Court Gardens Old and New*, designed and laid out the Elizabethan Knot Garden on the east front below the windows of the old Tudor buildings where they join the end of Wren's east façade. The patterns were based on the Knot Garden which Law had previously laid out in Stratford-on-Avon, but as Law himself wrote, 'The patterns of the interlacing bands or "ribbons" are taken entirely from those designed and published by the old masters on gardening of the time of Elizabeth and James I. The interspaces are planted with such old English flowers as tulips, hyacinths, daffodils, etc.' The small garden is surrounded by a hedge of dwarf box, and the intertwined bands are a variety of herbs – thyme, lavender, cotton-lavender, box and savory – and enclose clusters of brightly mixed flowers. As well as the traditional flowers, blooms such as begonias, unknown to the creators of sixteenth-century knot gardens, have more recently been added.

The Privy Garden:
looking back to the south front of the palace along the central path walled by sombre yews

Shortly after the Knot Garden was revived the old Tilt Yard Gardens, which William III had made into six kitchen gardens, and which were subsequently rented to market gardeners, were reclaimed by the palace. The gardens are still divided and, enclosed by old brick walls, have an air of independence from the rest of the grounds, although their proximity to the Tudor part of the palace is a constant reminder of their origin. Closest to the palace is a large rose garden with formally arranged beds, divided by grass paths, and narrow borders below the walls. The various beds contain massed mixed Hybrid Tea roses or mixed Floribundae, the centres being filled by larger shrub roses.

The surviving Tilt Tower has now been extended into a cafeteria and looks on to lawns shaded by a variety of mature trees – acacia, metasequoia, plane, and a Tulip tree – as well as smaller acers, cherries and a young 'Blue Spruce'. Amongst the trees stands a sundial which tells of an old connection. It came from the nearby villa of David Garrick, and bears the inscription:

> *David and Eva Garrick 1765*
> *Hampton-on-Thames*
> *Ut Umbra Sic Vita*

On the dial are the words '*Watch faster . . . Watch slower . . .*' Beyond, in a neighbouring part of the walled gardens, is an area of rich herbaceous plants mixed in energetic growth: campanulas, phlox and michaelmas daisies, delphiniums, dahlias and helleniums.

Beside the Tilt Yard Gardens the Wilderness has lost all traces of the formality with which it was devised by London and Wise, save only for the Maze, whose intricacies confound countless visitors every year. Beyond the Lion Gates from the Maze is the Laburnum Walk, a long metal pergola which in early summer becomes a tunnel dripping with golden-yellow trellised flowers. In these parts of the gardens the presence of the palace buildings is hardly felt, but on entering the Great Fountain Garden an awareness of spacious grandeur returns.

Despite the changes in the contents of the Great Fountain Garden this sense of grandeur has been maintained since William III first conceived his parterre as a focal-point for the lime avenues fit to lie beneath the windows of his new east front. The yew trees forming the apex of Charles II's *patte d'oie* are no longer trim narrow obelisks, but despite having grown to a size which partially obscures the original pattern they have, at the same time, assumed a formidable presence of their own, and now dominate the Great Fountain Garden in an unforgettable manner. Spaced out around the perimeter of the lawns of the main parterre and in the two wings are flower-beds that are filled in the spring and early summer with displays of massed tulips – each of the larger beds holding two thousand plants – and later on with a luxurious variety of summer bedding plants. Along the Broad Walk the two main herbaceous borders stretch into the

The Privy Garden:
leading to the old Thames-side entrance of the gardens with water meadows beyond;

distance: on one side from the palace to the river, and on the other from the gate into the Wilderness down to the Flower-Pot Gates. The plants in the Broad Walk borders are changed bi-annually, and in the narrow border in front of the tennis court and the small quadrangle known as Lady Mornington's Garden (named after the Duke of Wellington's mother who had rooms in this part of the palace) they are changed every year.

By the south-east corner of the palace a gateway leads to the Privy Garden with, on one side Queen Mary's Terrace and on the other, Queen Mary's Bower. From William and Mary's sundial on the south terrace the Privy Garden is divided by a yew avenue leading to the far end and Tijou's screen by the river. On each side of this avenue, between the overhanging branches of flowering trees and shrubs, grass paths wend past secluded statues. Two of these, nearest the palace, were made by Robert Jackson in 1869 and depict Spring and Autumn. At the far end of the garden, where it was intended to place corresponding statues of Summer and Winter, stand female figures cast in lead.

The Pond Gardens, which lie between the Orangery and the Banqueting House and are enclosed by low sixteenth-century walls and hedges, retain the intimacy of their original Tudor creation. In the larger, three tiers of brilliantly coloured bedding plants surround the central pond and the regular patterns of diminishing rectangles made by lawns and flagstone paths contrast with the figures of clipped box and yew. At the far end a lead statue of Venus is hidden within the canopy of her yew arbour. The smaller Pond Garden is sunken as it originally was, and its intricate pattern of formal detail has been reconstructed in the seventeenth-century manner. In its small parterre the single-jet fountain is surrounded by fleur-de-lys design of box-surrounded flower-beds. The low sixteenth-century walls enclosing this pattern are lined with closely clipped yew hedges, and the whole is an intriguing miniature.

The variety of Hampton Court is a result of its four hundred and fifty years of history. The people and events, the changes and continuities which have moulded its development combine to give the palace a mixed personality of both antiquity and timelessness. No longer subject to personal whim or ambition, and despite its sad absence from the centre stage of State, Hampton Court somehow continues to be a symbol of the monarchy, and its gardens, parks and buildings a pageant of their Royal past.

The Three Graces, silhouetted against the grandiose view of the park originally planned for Charles II

BUCKINGHAM PALACE
London

DURING THE LAST CENTURY Buckingham Palace has become in the eyes of the public the home of the monarchy. But behind the public façade: the Victoria Memorial, the Changing of the Guard, Royal appearances on the balcony and the long east front of Portland stone confronting the plane avenue of The Mall, behind the central quadrangle and Nash's honey-coloured west front, lies the oasis of Buckingham Palace's gardens. Few of the people travelling along Constitution Hill, Grosvenor Place or Buckingham Gate, which enclose the gardens, realize that behind the surrounding walls there exists in the heart of central London a unique 40-acre private garden. Only the canopy of trees rising above the walls gives the passer-by a hint of what lies beyond.

Part of the present Buckingham Palace gardens was a cultivated area some years before there was ever a house on the site – cultivated as a result of King James I's ambition to start up a silk industry in England shortly after his accession in 1603. Silk manufacturing had been established in France during the sixteenth century and by the reign of Henry IV was a thriving industry there. A desire to compete, combined with dreams of a new source of national wealth for whose establishment he could take credit, formed the basis of James I's ambitions. Vital to the success of a silk industry were the mulberry trees on which silk worms fed; after sending a despatch to all his Lord Lieutenants, urging them to plant the trees and help expand the production, the King paid William Stallenge £935 in 1609 for: 'The charge of four acres taken in for His Majesty's use, near to his palace of Westminster, for the planting of mulberry trees, together with the charge of walling, bevelling and planting thereof with mulberry trees etc according to an estimate thereof, subscribed by the surveyors of

Opposite: Public and private domain: the Wellington Arch seen through flowering cherries at the top end of the garden

His Majesty's works and the said William Stallenge'.

The four acres adjoined St James's Park which Henry VIII had enclosed for hunting from his new palace of St James's, built on the site of a twelfth-century hospital dedicated to St James. James I's determination for the success of his new venture was quite fervent, but whether through ignorance or carelessness it was doomed from the outset. The initial shortage of mulberry leaves for the silk worms to feed on was believed to be the problem but it proved to be far more fundamental. For the tree greatly preferred by the obviously discriminating silk worms is the 'White Mulberry' (*Morus alba*), while those that James I planted in thousands were the 'Black Mulberry (*Morus nigra*). Although the latter produces delicious black fruit, its leaves are not at all condusive to the production of silk.

The death of James I did not bring this fiasco to an end – Charles I inherited what was becoming a rather expensive white elephant. In 1628 charge of the Mulberry Garden passed from William Stallenge's son to Lord Aston, but Royal interest and faith in the project were dwindling. In 1640 the lease of the garden was sold to Lord Goring, who in 1633 had bought a piece of land on the south-west side of the garden and enlarged its existing house which had recently been built by a certain William Blake. It appears that Goring's house (which faced south, unlike subsequent ones which have faced east), had other grounds than the Mulberry Garden, including a bowling-alley, a 'wilderness' or maze, a fountain and a terrace; so from sometime around 1640 the Mulberry Garden became a public pleasure garden. Goring, who had become Earl of Norwich in 1646, was an ardent Royalist – he once wrote to his wife, 'Had I millions of crowns or scores of sons, the King and his cause should have them all' – and spent most of the years of the Second Civil War in exile with Charles II. The diarist, John Evelyn, gives an idea of the progress of the Mulberry Garden, writing in 1654, 'My Lady Gerrard treated us at Mulberry Garden, now the only place of refreshment about the town for persons of the best quality to be exceedingly cheated at; Cromwell and his partisans having shut and seized on Spring Gardens, which, till now, have been the usual rendezvous for the ladies and gallants of this season.' By the time of Charles II's restoration in 1660 the gardens were more popular than ever.

Goring died in 1662, having spent nearly all his considerable wealth in the cause of the King, and was able to leave only £450 per annum to his heir. He had been unable to regain the ownership of his property in London because of the various tenures during his exile, but notwithstanding the wrangles over possession, the Mulberry Garden thrived as a haunt of fashionable Londoners. Amongst the mulberry avenues the air was vibrant with gossip and arbours hid the illegal assignations which typified the lightly-held morals of the age. Sir Charles Sedley, a popular and notoriously risqué dramatist, set one of his plays there, calling it *The*

Mulberry Garden, in which a conversation between a group of men reflects the prevalent mood!

Estridge: 'Come, drink a glass round.'

Modish: 'I can't get down a drop of this wine more without a frolic.'

Wildish: 'Every man name the woman that has obliged him last, and drink all their healths in a brimmer.'

Modish: 'Content; begin Estridge.'

Estridge: 'Olivia. Now Modish, name yours.'

Modish: 'Victoria, Victoria. We must have your person too, Wildish.'

Wildish: 'Mrs Betty.'

Such scenes are described in a number of other plays of the period and show the pleasures to be enjoyed by young bloods. Samuel Pepys had little time for them and wrote after his first visit to the gardens, 'A very silly place, worse than Spring Gardens, and but little company, and those of a rascally, whoring, roguing sort of people, only a wilderness, that is somewhat pretty, but rude. Did not stay to drink.'

Henry Bennet, Earl of Arlington, had bought Goring House in 1664. Arlington was one of the foremost figures of the Restoration court and it was he who brought Goring House into the centre of political and social affairs, establishing it as one of London's leading houses. Distinguished by the strip of black plaster which he always wore over a scar across his nose, Arlington was one of the main members of the 'Cabal' – the group which for a time dominated Restoration politics – and was the chief rival to George Villiers, 2nd Duke of Buckingham for the King's favour. Outside politics, his extravagance and love of entertaining, which his wife shared, were legendary. He was reported to have more carriages in his mews than any other nobleman and to employ over a thousand servants at Goring House and Euston Hall, his palatial seat in Suffolk. Goring House clearly benefited enormously from his extravagance, for Evelyn recorded after visiting there in 1665, shortly after Arlington had acquired it, 'Went to Goring House, now Mr Secretary Bennet's, ill-built, but the place capable of being made a pretty villa.' By the 1670s Arlington had filled the house with numerous treasures in whose collection he spared no effort or expenditure, and in 1673 Evelyn was writing, 'She [Lady Arlington] carried us up into her new dressing-room at Goring House, where was a bed ... and other so rich furniture as I had seldom seen: to this excess of superfluity were we now arrived, and that not only at Court, but almost universally, even to wantonness and profusion.'

Only to a man of Arlington's means and insatiable appetite would the destruction of his house and its priceless contents by fire in 1674 have meant not irrevocable disaster but the opportunity to rebuild on a far grander scale. The fire followed shortly after his attempted impeachment by the House of Commons, as a result of which Arlington began gradually to withdraw from the political arena and to concentrate his attention on his new house, its contents and surroundings. Whatever people's varying opinions, the popularity of the Mulberry Garden had by that time waned and Arlington acquired its lease in 1675. His new house was called Arlington House and received a rapturous reception from Arlington's protégé, the poet John Dryden, in the form of a Latin poem. The poem is of particular interest as it describes the new gardens at considerable length; extracts reveal the apparent paradise which Arlington laid out around his new mansion:

'Thy beauteous gardens charm the ravish'd sight,
And surfeit every sense with soft delight;
Where-e'er we turn our still transported eyes,
New scenes of Art with Nature join'd arise;
We dwell indulgent on the lovely scene,
The lengthen'd vista or the carpet green;
A thousand graces bless th' inchanted ground,
And throw promiscuous beauties all around.

Within thy fair parterres appear to view
A thousand flowers of various form and hue
There spotless lilies rear their sickly heads,
And purple violets creep along the beds;
Here shews the bright jonquil its gilded face,
Join'd with the pale carnation's fairer grace;
The painted tulip and the blushing rose
A blooming wilderness of sweets compose.

In such a scene great Cupid wounded lay,
To Love and Psyche's charms a glorious prey,
Here felt the pleasing pain and thrilling smart,
And prov'd too well his own resistless dart.

High in the midst appears a rising ground,
With greens and balustrades inclos'd around;
Here a new wonder stops the wandering sight,
A dome whose walls and roof transmit the light;
Here foreign plants and trees exotic thrive,
And in the cold unfriendly climate live;
For when bleak Winter chills the rolling year,
The guarded strangers find their safety here;
And, fenc'd from storms and the inclement air,
They sweetly flourish ever green and fair;
Their lively buds they shot, and blossoms show,
And gaily bloom amidst surrounding snow . . .

A curious terrace stops the wandering eye,
Where lovely jasmines fragrant shade supply:
Whose tender branches, in their pride array'd,
Invite the wanderer to the grateful shade.'

After 1681, when Arlington bought the upper and lower Crow Fields from Sir Thomas Grosvenor for £3500, which lie to the north-west of the old

Mulberry Garden, his land covered most of the site of the present Buckingham Palace gardens.

Despite his declining influence in politics and at court, Arlington had the great satisfaction of seeing his only daughter, Lady Isabella Bennet, married to Henry FitzRoy, Duke of Grafton, Charles II's bastard son by Barbara Villiers, Duchess of Cleveland. During the last years of his life Arlington continued to embellish his house for his adored heiress until his death in 1685. But it does not seem that after all his work on her behalf his daughter occupied Arlington House for very long, for shortly after the death of her husband in 1690 Stow records in his *Survey* of the cities of London and Westminster: 'At the upper end of the Park westward is Arlington House ... it is a most neat Box, and sweetly sealed amongst gardens, beside the prospect of the Park, and the adjoining fields. At present the Duke of Devonshire resideth here as Tenant of the Duchess of Grafton.' At the same time another description gives greater detail of part of the gardens: 'Arlington House, being now in the hands of my Lord of Devonshire, is a fair place with good walks, both airy and shady. There are six of the greatest earthen pots that are anywhere else, being at least ten feet over within the edge, but they stand abroad, and have nothing in them but the tree holy-oke, an indifferent plant which grows well enough in the ground. Their greenhouse is very well and their green-yard excels, but their greens are not so bright and clean as farther off in the country, as if they suffered something from the smutty air of the town.'

At some stage during Devonshire's tenancy the Duchess of Grafton sold Arlington House to John Sheffield, 3rd Earl of Mulgrave. He had courted the Princess Anne for which he had suffered at the hand of Charles II, losing his position of favour with the King, and, it is alleged, being sent to the siege of Tangiers in a ship full of holes designed to sink during the journey. However, he survived both the trip and the subsequent loss of the throne by the Stuarts to William of Orange, becoming Marquess of Normanby in 1694 and finally, regaining complete favour on Queen Anne's succession, he was created Duke of Buckingham in 1703. (The confusion in previous books about Buckingham Palace over whether Sheffield was made Duke of Buckingham or Buckinghamshire can safely be attributed to the fact that his full title was 'Duke of the County of Buckingham'.) Thus, assured of both power and wealth, in that year Buckingham demolished Arlington House (which had anyway been damaged by fire during the Duke of Devonshire's tenancy), and in its place built a yet more impressive house, suitably re-named Buckingham House.

The new house was designed by William Talman and built by William Winde. In its positioning Buckingham showed what terms of familiarity he enjoyed with Queen Anne, but at the same time incurred her severe displeasure. Upon his request to expand his property the Queen leased her favourite a small part of St James's Park – '2 rods and 9 perches' – but Buckingham greedily helped himself to more than this, despite a severe note of complaint from the Queen which he chose to ignore. Thus he was able to build his house so that it looked straight down The Mall as well as dominating the main avenues and canal of the park. The completed building received numerous comments, favourable and unfavourable, and Edward Hatton in his *New View of London* (1708) noted prophetically that it was, 'a site not to be contemned by the greatest monarch'. The most detailed account is a letter which Buckingham himself wrote to the Duke of Shrewsbury, whose pages lead the reader through the rooms and grounds of the new house, describing the events which filled Buckingham's day.

'. . . For though my garden is such as, by not pretending to rarities or curiosities, has nothing in it to inveigh one's thoughts, yet by the advantage of situation and prospect it is able to suggest the noblest that can be, in presenting at once to view a vast Town, a Palace, and a magnificent Cathedral . . .

'The avenues to the house are along St James's Park, through rows of goodly elms on one hand and gay flourishing limes on the other, that for coaches, this for walking; with the Mall lying between them. This reaches to my iron palisade that incompasses a square court, which has in its midst a great basin with statues and water works, and from its entrance, rises all the way imperceptibly till we mount to a Terrace in front of a large Hall . . .

'To these gardens we go down from the house by seven steps, into a gravel walk that reaches across the whole garden, with a covered arbour at each end of it. Another of 30-foot broad leads from the front of the house, and lies between two groves of tall lime trees planted in several equal ranks upon a carpet of grass; the outsides of these groves are bordered with tubs of Bays and Orange-trees.

'At the end of this broad walk, you go up to a Terrace 400 paces long, with a large Semicircle in the middle from whence is beheld the Queen's two parks, and a great part of Surrey; then going down a few steps you walk on the banks of a canal 600 yards long, and 17 broad, with two rows of limes on each side.

'On one side of this Terrace a Wall covered with Roses and Jassemines is made low to admit the view of a meadow full of cattle just under it, (no disagreeable object in the midst of a great City) and at each end a descent into parterres with fountains and water-works.

'From the biggest of these parterres we pass into a little square garden that has a fountain in the middle, and two green houses on the sides, with a convenient bathing apartment in one of them, and near another part of it lies a flower garden. Below all this a kitchen-garden full of the best sorts of fruit, has several walks in it for the coldest of weather . . .'

The gardens of Buckingham House, laid out by Henry Wise for the Duke of Buckingham at a cost of £1,000. An eighteenth-century plan attributed to Bridgeman

The gardens which Buckingham described in such exhaustive detail were laid out for him by Henry Wise at a cost of £1000 and would appear to have incorporated most of the features of the time. Buckingham was

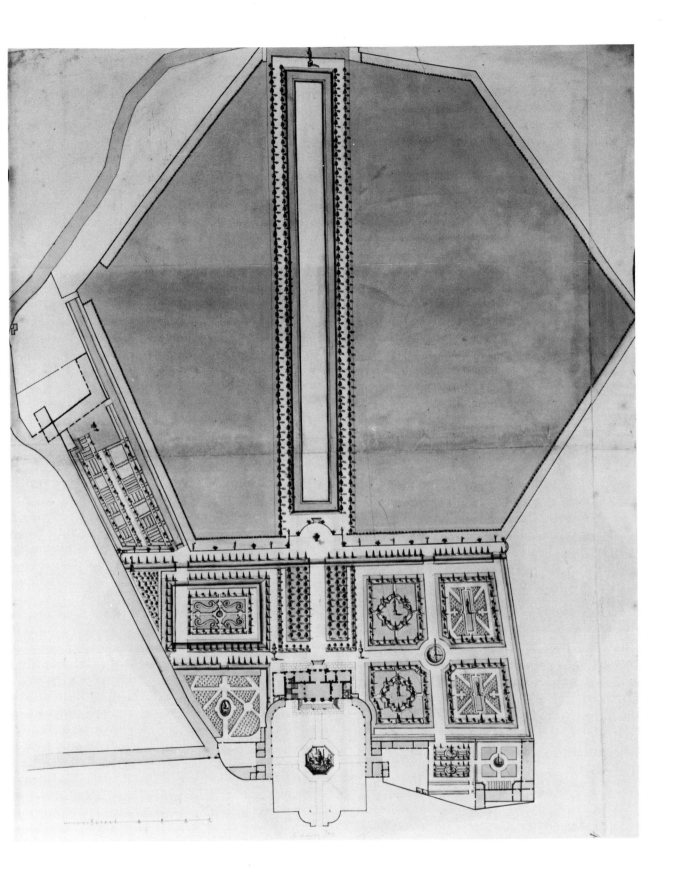

clearly, and justifiably, proud of his magnificent new house, and decorated each of the four façades with bold Latin inscriptions. Over the main entrance on the east side were the words, '*Sic Siti Laetantur Lares*', whose translation reveals the blend of supreme self-confidence and arrogance possessed by those members of the aristocracy who had achieved such heights as Buckingham: 'The Household Gods delight in such a situation.' It was the situation of the house, prominently in the public eye, which led to the numerous contemporary satires written about it, the most succinct of which was found pinned to the gates of the courtyard one morning: 'This is the house that Jack built.' The Duke was supposed to have answered the sarcastic joke by saying he would rather be the author of that witty line than master of the whole structure.

Buckingham's personality typified those aristocrats of his time who used their privileged position and personal qualities to the full, and the scope of his activities and interests was enormous – soldier, politician, courtier, builder and gardener, avid collector of objects of artistic beauty and value, poet and bibliophile, compulsive gambler and philanderer. He died in 1721, having retired some years earlier from politics and court life – George II disliked him intensely – to spend his days peacefully enjoying the pleasures of 'Buck' House, which on his death passed to his equally remarkable wife.

Catherine, Duchess of Buckingham, was born Catherine Darnley, illegitimate daughter of James II by Catherine Sedley – herself the illegitimate daughter of the author of *The Mulberry Garden*, Sir Charles Sedley. The surname Darnley derived from her great-great-grandfather, the ill-fated husband of Mary Queen of Scots. Albeit as a bastard the Duchess brought continuity to the story of Buckingham House, being the great-granddaughter of James I who had planted his famous mulberry trees one hundred years earlier, and a first cousin of the Duke of Grafton who had married Arlington's daughter, Lady Isabella Bennet. Her semi-royal descent gave the Duchess excessive delusions of grandeur. Horace Walpole, who referred to the Duchess as 'Princess Buckingham' recorded numerous amusing tales at her expense, including one of a visit by the Duchess to the opera, and the scene of her death-bed: 'The Duchess of Buckingham, who is more mad with pride than any mercer's wife in Bedlam, came the other night to the opera *en princesse*, literally in robes of red velvet and ermine . . . Princess Buckingham is dead or dying. She sent for Mr Anstis and settled the ceremonial of her burial. On Saturday she was so ill that she feared dying before the pomp was come home . . . But yesterday was the greatest stroke of all. She made her ladies vow to her that if she should lie senseless, they would not sit down in the room before she was dead.' In fact, after a suitable period of lying-in-state at Buckingham House, her husband was buried in Westminster Abbey – where she later joined him – after a funeral of enormous pomp, only exceeded by the ceremony of her own. Their only surviving son Edmund, 2nd Duke of

Buckingham, was not even allowed the request in his will to be buried in the gardens of Buckingham House, for he also was thrust, unwillingly, into a tomb in the Abbey.

As well as providing unlimited scope for humour on account of her preposterous eccentricity, in 1723 the Duchess received the first Royal attempt to buy Buckingham House. It came from the Prince of Wales (later George II). Her reply was utterly characteristic: 'If their Royal Highnesses will have everything stand as it does, furniture and pictures, I will have £3000 per annum, both run hazard of being spoiled, and the last, to be sure, will be all to be bought new whenever my son is of age. The quantity the rooms take cannot be well furnished under £10,000; but if their Highnesses will permit the pictures all to be removed, and buy the furniture as it will be valued by different people, the house shall go at £2000 – If the Prince and Princess prefer the buying outright, under £60,000 it will not be parted with as it now stands, and all His Majesty's revenue cannot purchase a place so fit for them nor for a less sum – The Princess asked me at the drawing room if I would sell my fine house. I answered her smiling, that I was under no necessity to part with it; yet, when what I thought was the value of it should be offered, perhaps my prudence might overcome my inclination.' The terms contained in the Duchess's haughty reply were rejected and she remained at Buckingham House until her death in 1742. But because neither she nor her husband left a legitimate heir – the aforesaid Edmund had died in Rome without an heir, and with his death the family's titles became extinct – Buckingham House, together with the other Buckingham estates, passed to Charles Herbert, Buckingham's illegitimate son. Buckingham had laid down in his will that should Herbert inherit the property he must change his name to Sheffield. Possibly Sheffield was unnerved by the splendour of his new surroundings. Certainly the Royal surveyors were well aware that his father's house stood partially on illegally taken Crown land and that the old lease of the Mulberry Garden granted to Arlington was due to expire in 1771. So in 1762, after the Monarchy had been somewhat overshadowed for some time at St James's Palace by its palatial neighbour, Sheffield sold the house and its grounds for £28,000, to George III, who two years earlier had succeeded to the throne and married Queen Charlotte.

Thus the Royal Family acquired the site with which they had been involved ever since James I's Mulberry Garden, by virtue of their partial ownership of its grounds and its position on the edge of the Royal domain of St James's Park. After the 1st Duke of Buckingham had finished building it was clear that Buckingham House rather than St James's Palace dominated the park and indeed the whole area linking the old cities of Westminster and London – a position as potentially intolerable as in reality Wolsey's palace at Hampton Court had been to Henry VIII.

George III and Queen Charlotte were delighted with their new home and during the early years of the King's reign spent much of the year there. They made a number of alterations to the interior of the house, redecorating many of the rooms and bringing in paintings from other Royal residences – such as the Raphael cartoons from Hampton Court – and commissioning new marble fireplaces, furniture etc. The most significant additions were the paintings which George III bought from Consul Joseph Smith in 1765. Smith had been the Consul in Venice during which time he had both collected and commissioned a rare selection of paintings – among the commissions were the drawings and paintings by Canaletto now in the Royal collection – which now adorned the walls of Buckingham House. As well as alterations to the interior of the house additions were also made to the actual buildings; behind the curving colonnades on the garden front the wings on either side of the main courtyard were linked to the central block of the house. Here George III made his library to which he was continually adding. His collecting started because in 1757 George II had given the old Royal Library to the recently-founded British Museum. The library was often visited by Samuel Johnson who was impressed enough to remark that there were books, 'more numerous and curious than he supposed any person could have made in the time which the King had employed'.

During these early years George III and Queen Charlotte enjoyed the simple domesticity of their private life at Buckingham House, retaining St James's Palace for more formal and state functions. For the Queen, especially, the gardens were a particularly enjoyable part of their new home, and Henry Wise's work for the 1st Duke of Buckingham was left largely unchanged. Queen Charlotte did add a flower garden; she concentrated on growing carnations which were among her favourite flowers, and the gardens gained two somewhat exotic novelties in the form of a zebra and an elephant, known as 'the Queen's animals', they were objects of great fascination to the public who could watch them grazing in their paddock.

In honour of the King's birthday in 1763, when most of the initial improvements to the house were nearing completion, Queen Charlotte planned a celebration which was a forerunner of the *fêtes champêtres* she was later to enjoy organizing at Frogmore. The King was kept in ignorance of the preparations until the evening of the party, when Queen Charlotte led him to the window of her Japan Room to view the spectacular scene in the garden. Lit up by thousands of glass lamps were a temple and bridge, which had been specially built for the occasion, and in front of them a huge transparency of the King, similarly illuminated, depicted him giving peace to all the world with, at his feet, trophies of British conquests and the falling figures of various evils such as Envy and Malice.

In 1775 the house was settled on Queen Charlotte by Act of

Parliament and became known as 'The Queen's House'. However, as Kew and Windsor began steadily to hold greater attractions for the King and Queen, their visits to their London home became less frequent. The gardens of the Queen's House never received the attention from Queen Charlotte which those at Kew, and more especially Frogmore, did, and by the last years of his reign, when the King was almost constantly at Windsor, the house became more and more the official London residence rather than the private home it had been during the early years of their marriage. A factor which contributed to the Royal preference for the more rural environments of Kew and Windsor was the steady encroachment of London upon the grounds of the Queen's House, thereby diminishing the possibility of privacy.

George IV acceded in 1820, after nearly two decades as Prince Regent. During these years he had become increasingly unpopular because of the extravagance of his building projects – the Royal Pavilion at Brighton and Carlton House at the far end of The Mall from the Queen's House. (He had inherited the latter on the death of Queen Charlotte in 1818.) By 1825, in the face of enraged criticism on every side, it was quite clear that he intended to build a new palace for himself to replace the Queen's House. By deceiving Parliament into granting the necessary initial sum of money, supposedly to start work on urgent repairs, George IV had enabled his architect, John Nash, to pull the old house down and begin what was to be the fourth house built on the site within a hundred and fifty years.

While the new palace was being built George IV swept away Wise's formal gardens and employed William Townsend Aiton (who had previously taken over charge of the gardens at Kew from his father) to landscape the grounds. In place of the old parterres, avenues and flower-beds, a new terrace, the length of the garden front of Nash's building, led down to a huge sweep of lawn. Beyond, Aiton joined the existing two ponds together and enlarged them into the present lake, removing the excavated earth to form the mound on the south-west side of the gardens.

In the light of the King's previous extravagances and the depressed economic climate after the Napoleonic Wars, both the new palace and gardens were greeted with widespread condemnation and derision as they took shape. It was the bitter satire continually aimed at the King during these years which led him to withdraw more and more, first to Brighton and then to the Royal Lodge in Windsor Park. An illustrated poem by T. Hume, which appeared around 1829, typifies the attacks on the King and Buckingham Palace (as the new house came to be called, in preference to other possibilities, serious or sarcastic – St George's Palace, Pimlico Palace, the New Palace or the King's House). The poem, entitled 'The House that N—H Built', is full of venomous wit, and at one stage the poet turns his attention to the gardens:

Overleaf: Nash's west front seen from across the lake; in this unlikely setting the exotic flamingoes look surprisingly at home

'To rail at the Palace and Triumphal Arch,
Which, 'tis said, will be probably finished in March,
(And, compared with the elegant gates of Hyde Park,
May justly be term'd tasteless, gloomy and dark),
Which leads to the large Pond of Water, or Basin,
Where the Royal Narcissus may see his dear face in,
Ere he rove 'mongst the Pyramids, Temples, and Ditches,
Where Naiads and Cupids are seen without breeches,
(*For such things in West are allow'd, and thought pretty,*
Though Venus and Cupids daren't go in the City),
Who preside o'er the Fountains, the Promenades, and Rides,
(And 'twould puzzle old Harry to tell what besides),
Which lead from the Hill, the magnificent Mound,
Thrown up in the garden, full half a mile round,
Thickly planted with trees, and as high as a steeple,
To protect from the breeze and hide from the people –. . . .'

Despite the attacks and subsequent alterations to the buildings, Nash's golden west façade of Bath stone survives today and, with the other projects he carried out for George IV, is part of their major contribution to the architecture of London; and it is Aiton's landscape which is the basis of the present gardens. Although George IV took the characteristic step of planting screening belts of trees around the perimeter of the grounds he died in 1830 before the palace was complete and his brother, the bluff, eccentric, Duke of Clarence, became King William IV, inheriting as well – extremely unwillingly – the enormous edifice. He spent much of his short reign putting forward reasons why he should not live there, and when the Houses of Parliament were burnt down in 1834 immediately offered Buckingham Palace as a replacement. However, during the 1830s the architect Edward Blore was called in to complete the palace. The work included finishing the triumphal arch which George IV had set up in the courtyard as the main entrance to the palace. George IV had been inspired by Constantine's Arch in Rome to which it is similar. The arch never received the trappings of marble and bronze figures, bas reliefs and ornamental gates which George IV had intended, and in 1851 it was removed to its present site, on the north-eastern edge of Hyde Park; Marble Arch, is, of course, one of the landmarks of central London. Criticism of the palace continued during William IV's reign, although one account does show grudging admiration for the views over St James's Park and the gardens: 'The park itself has been greatly improved, its interior having been metamorphosed from a meadow with a formal, dingy canal intersecting it, into a cheerful and tolerably picturesque pleasure-ground. The gardens at the back of the Palace have been improved quite in equal degree, so that either way the view from the windows must be sufficiently agreeable –, nay, in this respect, perhaps the Palace has no cause to envy any other building of the kind in any European capital.'

One of the illustrations
from the viciously satirical
poem
'The House that
N——H Built', by T.
  Hume –
'. . . Which leads to the
  large Pond of Water or
  Basin, Where the Royal
  Narcissus may see his
  dear face in . . .'
The giraffe was a gift to
George IV from
Mohammed Ali, the
Pasha of Egypt

Edward Blore continued his work on the palace during the early years of Queen Victoria's reign, for shortly after her accession in 1837 the young Queen decided to make her uncle's unpopular palace her main London home. By 1847 Blore had removed Nash's dome – which had been the main object of ridicule and criticism – and the four towers along the garden front, as well as refacing the east front. The changes emerging in the gardens were characteristic of Queen Victoria's influence, and later, her husband's. Thick shrubberies and flower parterres broke up the sweeping nature of Aiton's landscape. However, Queen Victoria's interest in the gardens of her homes derived not so much from horticultural enthusiasm as from her enjoyment of beautiful surroundings; and fundamental to this enjoyment was the amount of privacy which the gardens afforded her and Prince Albert. As at Frogmore, the lake in the Buckingham Palace gardens allowed Prince Albert to demonstrate his prowess at skating, a skill which, like his other abilities, received the rapturous admiration of Queen Victoria.

The most interesting addition to the gardens by Queen Victoria and Prince Albert had been the Comus Pavilion, built in 1844. The design of the pavilion was by Ludwig Grüner (who also designed the Mausoleum at Frogmore), and although partly inspired by neo-Gothic romanticism it was reported to be, 'picturesque and fantastic, without any style of architecture', in a book by John Murray entitled *Her Majesty's Pavilion in Buckingham Palace Gardens*. The pavilion's name derived from the decoration of the interior, carried out by eight leading members of the Royal Academy, and depicting scenes from Milton's *Comus*. Positioned on the top of the mound, close to the Grosvenor Place side of the gardens, the pavilion – like the tea-house at Frogmore – provided Queen Victoria with a garden-house where she could work at her papers. It was a sad loss when the pavilion had to be pulled down in 1928, having become derelict during the First World War.

By the 1850s a growing desire to be away from London as much as possible had led the Queen and her husband to Osborne and Balmoral, and the attractions of their Buckingham Palace gardens suffered from the far greater scope of these rivals for seclusion. After the Prince Consort's death in 1861 Queen Victoria's withdrawal resulted in almost total desertion of the palace and allowed the gardens to become extensively overgrown. It was typical of Queen Victoria that in 1881, having discussed a plan to clear and re-plant some of the most unmanageable shrubberies there, she suddenly stopped the work, saying that the gardens were well planned and quite tidy and that above all there were to be no alterations, as these would involve the removal of signs of the Prince Consort's work. During the last years of her reign Queen Victoria did return to London, and to Buckingham Palace on occasions, by which time she was such a revered figure in the eyes of her people that they were prepared to forget her years of absence.

Edward VII brought to the gardens their most unusual, and to many eyes, their most beautiful ornaments, the pair of Japanese bronze cranes with which he was presented in India at the Delhi Durbar of 1903. Supremely graceful, the birds bring a note of uncommon variety to the banks of the lake.

Also unusual, partly because of its bewildering size, is the Waterloo Vase, which stands in an opening partly surrounded by a variety of trees, including the *Taxodium distichum*. The vase stands 15 feet high and is one of the largest objects in the world to be carved out of a single piece of marble. It is supposed to have been made on orders from Napoleon Bonaparte for his sister, Elisa Bacciochi, whom he had made ruler of the Principality of Lucca, and the marble came from Carrara in Lucca. After Napoleon's defeat Louis XVIII offered the vase to the Prince Regent, who accepted it with alacrity; but William IV was unappreciative of its beauty and presented it to the new National Gallery. Finally the enormous ornament came to rest in the Buckingham Palace gardens in 1907, when the Trustees of the National Gallery offered it to Edward VII.

Shortly before the First World War Buckingham Palace received its final major structural alteration, the re-facing of Blore's east front to the rather dull design by Sir Aston Webb RA. The work was swiftly completed and soon the palace was showing its dreary grey façade of Portland stone to the newly-erected Victoria Memorial. Nearly three hundred years after the first house had appeared on the site the series of architectural changes which had been presented to Londoners ended and,

looking at the west front today, it has an air of permanence which belies the number of its predecessors. Repairs had to be made when the fabric was badly damaged by bombs during the Second World War but mercifully, despite the determined efforts of German pilots, the palace survived scarred but not mortally wounded.

The buildings of the palace may have achieved permanence, but change and progress never stop in a garden and Buckingham Palace gardens are no exception. After the First World War King George V and

Crocuses on the lawns which were part of George IV's sweeping changes. In contrast, a more recent set-piece display of camellias has replaced the Victorian shrubberies

Queen Mary revived and expanded the garden parties which had been initiated by Queen Victoria, and they continue today as a major part of the Royal summer season, to the delight of the thousands of people who are invited and thus gain a privileged glimpse of these private gardens. And as with the Royal gardens in general one of the immediate impressions is the balance between the legacies of the past and more recent changes. Over the years Nash's west façade has retained its Georgian harmony; and the view from the wide terrace continues to be dominated by the great sweep of lawn leading to the lake, with the balustrade of Coade stone surmounted by elaborately carved Coade stone urns dividing the terrace from the garden. The terrace is the ideal launching-off point for the visitor – from here he can gain a picture of the whole before descending to the lawn and beyond, where the varied style of the different areas is revealed.

The reign of King George VI saw many of the dense Victorian shrubberies being cleared or thinned and in their places a wide selection of far more decorative flowering trees and shrubs planted. Their individual qualities of size, shape and colour make these ideally suited to such a large garden. Many of the ornamental trees are of species whose introduction from abroad since the late nineteenth century, and from the far East and America in particular, has transformed so many English gardens. As well as a variety of magnolias, camellias and rhododendrons – particular favourites of King George VI and Queen Elizabeth – there are a number of other specimens of flowering and decorative trees whose shades of colour brighten vistas which also contain the more mature native trees: planes, the outstanding trees for urban surroundings, and beeches. The *Sophora japonica*, 'Japanese Pagoda Tree', which defies its name and originates from China, gives a glorious display of cream-white flowers in late summer, while earlier in the year appear the contrasting tones of lilac-coloured flowers on the *Buddleia alternifolia* and *Paulownia tomentosa*. Most striking of the non-flowering trees are the acers, three of which show the variety this species can provide. The names of *Acer saccharinum* ('Silver Maple') and *Acer palmatum* Senkaki ('Coral Bark Maple') describe their colours, while *Acer palmatum atropurpureum* bears almost claret-coloured foliage.

Among the older trees two are most noteworthy for quite different reasons. The first, a lone mulberry standing in the south-west corner of the gardens, has obvious nostalgic links with the very earliest days of the gardens; but its age cannot match the sentimental assertions that it is one of James I's original trees. The other is a lofty *Taxodium distichum*, 'Swamp Cypress' whose sharply columnar shape is in strong contrast to the more spreading canopies of the other, deciduous, trees in the gardens.

Tall though many of the trees are, the privacy which the Royal Family look for in the gardens has been threatened by the hideous high-rise buildings which have so disfigured London's skyline in the last twenty-five years. One measure to combat this is the young avenue of *Aesculus indica*, 'Indian Horse Chestnuts', which curves away from the north-west corner of the terrace to the more secluded areas which lie between the perimeter of the lawn and the boundary wall. The choice of tree gives historical continuity, for two single specimens of the same horse chestnut with pink-flushed flowers, were planted by King George VI and Queen Elizabeth in 1937 to commemorate their coronation.

The young chestnut avenue leads to the long north side of the gardens, bounded by Constitution Hill, up which Charles II strode every morning for his daily exercise when he was at St James's Palace, no doubt looking with keen interest into Lord Arlington's gardens. Situated as it is near the

Royal Family's private entrance to the palace on the north front, this area, which partly covers the site of the old Mulberry Garden, contains many of the most interesting and enjoyable features of the present gardens. Close to the entrance from the forecourt and curving away towards an area of recent planting is a herbaceous border of suitably regal proportions – it is 175 yards long. Resounding colour appears in the border throughout the season: soon after the gentler presence of crocuses and daffodils, which are sprinkled throughout the gardens, come the gaudy ranks of closely-planted tulips, that seem to aspire to rival the traditional display at the same time on the Great Fountain Garden at Hampton Court. As the tulips come to an end the border is filled with herbaceous plants, its size allowing for a strikingly impressive array of luxurious quantities, with hardly a foot of earth through the summer months between the delphiniums, geraniums, crinums and a host of others. Following the path from the herbaceous border along behind a small summer-house and a mixed stand of trees planted over the years by the various Royal occupants of Buckingham Palace, the visitor needs the distant buzz of traffic beyond the wall to remind him that he is in London and not in the heart of the country – an illusion which is perhaps the gardens' most intriguing quality.

The lake, covering nearly four acres, stretches down from the cascade at the top end and around the island to the foot of the mound in the bottom corner of the gardens, and probably contributes more to their character than any other single feature. It is the lake and trees which successfully combat the regular shape and flatness of much of the gardens, and the partly unkempt naturalness of the lake's banks adds to the informality of the atmsophere. Edward VII's cranes share the lakeside with the equally – if not more – exotic flamingoes, who have the advantage of being fully animated despite the extreme unnaturalness of their surroundings. The flamingoes arrived in 1961 and continue the tradition of populating the gardens with startlingly unexpected creatures begun by Queen Charlotte with her elephant and zebra. No doubt they steer well clear of the Royal corgis. Rhododendrons and magnolias form a backcloth to the cascade, and among the waterside plants are the tropical-looking *Gunnera manicata*, and very aptly *Osmunda regalis*, the 'Royal Fern', whose name derives from the legend that Osmund, a king of ancient Britain, hid his daughter from the invading Danes amongst the dense foliage of this fern.

One might expect a garden temple called the Admiralty Summer House to stand overlooking or near the water, but in fact it is beyond the Waterloo Vase, close to the northern edge of the gardens. This classical building originally stood in the gardens of the Admiralty, but was presented to the Royal Family and moved to Buckingham Palace, at the beginning of this century. The Triton figures, which form its four pillars, look out on to the beds of the rose garden that girdles it with summer blooms. Among the Hybrid Tea varieties is the rose named after Queen

Elizabeth II's Silver Jubilee, and in other beds are a rich variety: Floribundae, such as the deliciously scented Pink Parfait; the *Rugosa* Blanc Double de Coubert – so white that at night it appears incandescent; the only pink, Nevada; the *Hybrid-moyesii* Margaret Hilling; the old-fashioned rose, 'Chapeau de Napoleon', so called because of its tricorn-shaped crown; and clustering over the pergola behind the summer house, the climber Madame Gregoire Staechlin.

In the top corner of the Buckingham Palace gardens, overlooked by the statue of the Wellington Arch, is the Grey Border, given to Queen Elizabeth II and the Duke of Edinburgh as a Silver Wedding present by Lord and Lady Astor of Hever. Here shades of grey and silver leaf and flower mix together, lavenders and silver thymes as well as *Artemisia palmeri* and *Senecio laxifolius*. Most of the plants are sun-loving and thrive in the south-facing aspect of the border.

Buckingham Palace has gathered its history over three-and-a-half centuries, and the present landscape has been maturing since the beginning of the nineteenth century. However, it is largely in the last fifty years that the gardens have acquired the wide variety of plants, shrubs and trees which they contain today, though many of the standard trees are considerably older. It is this combination of change and continuity that makes the gardens so interesting, and makes them more than merely gardens in which the Royal Family may relax in private or use for entertaining during the London season every summer.

The fifteen-foot tall Waterloo Vase, carved from a single block of Carrara marble, stands in isolated grandeur on the north lawn. Towering in the background is the splendid *Taxodium distichum*

BALMORAL

Aberdeenshire

IN THE SUMMER OF 1842, five years after her accession to the throne and two-and-a-half years after her marriage to Prince Albert of Saxe-Coburg and Gotha, Queen Victoria announced to her Prime Minister, Sir Robert Peel, her desire for him to make arrangements for Prince Albert and herself to spend an autumn holiday in Scotland. With Lord Melbourne's support his plans went ahead and the Royal party left London for Scotland by boat on 29 August. It was the enjoyment of this and two subsequent visits, in 1844 and 1847, that made Queen Victoria and her husband determined to acquire a home of their own in the Highlands, a quest which was fulfilled in 1848 when Prince Albert bought the remaining lease on Balmoral Castle.

Historically, Queen Victoria's desire to visit Scotland was unusual, and her determination to find a suitable home for regular autumn visits unprecedented. Other than a brief visit by King George IV to Edinburgh in 1822, no reigning monarch had been to Scotland since Charles I, over 200 years previously. During the eighteenth century relations between the monarchy and Scotland were severely strained by the two Jacobite uprisings of 1715 and 1745, and the Scots were full of bitterness after the brutalities of Culloden and the ensuing military rule. The situation improved with time, particularly as a result of the advances in communications and economic innovations of the Industrial Revolution, and also the active participation of Highland regiments in the British Army. George IV's trip to Edinburgh in 1822 was an undisputed success; but in the 1840s England and Scotland were still two very different worlds.

Queen Victoria's initial enthusiasm for Scotland, and indeed her husband's, developed with each visit into growing affection. Undaunted

Opposite: The south front of the castle and, beyond, the dense forests of Deeside

by the weather, even after travelling around the west coast in 1847 when it rained incessantly, they quickly succumbed to the spell of the scenery and atmosphere. They spent that autumn at Windsor in a mood of excited expectation at the possibility of finding a suitable home in the north. One weighty consideration was the climate, and advice at this point from Sir James Clark, the Queen's chief physician, helped settle the location; he mentioned that his son had been convalescing from an illness at Balmoral, the Deeside home of Sir Robert Gordon, where he had found not only sunshine but also an unusual purity and dryness in the air. In October that year Sir Robert died suddenly and his brother, the Earl of Aberdeen, suggested that Queen Victoria and Prince Albert take up the lease which still had twenty-seven years to run. After initial enquiries, they decided to do so, completing the agreement in February 1848, and they looked forward to their first visit to Deeside in the autumn of that year.

The early history of Balmoral contains many of the vicissitudes of family fortune which were typical of Scotland. Originally it was part of the Province of Mar, but in 1484 the first written mention of 'Bouchmorale' – one of a series of spellings of the name which evolved over the years – records that Sir Alexander Gordon leased the estate for £8 6s 8d per annum. Sir Alexander's home was at the old-established Abergeldie Castle, whose lands marched with Balmoral's and the combined estates made a firm footing on Deeside which the family enjoyed in security until the mid-seventeenth century. But by 1662 financial pressures, particularly from the Farquharsons of Inverey, who were demanding the payment of debts due, forced the Gordons to give up the estate of Balmoral which the Farquharsons – already very powerful at Invercauld nearby on north Deeside – immediately acquired.

Despite their local power as a clan the Farquharsons' tenure of Balmoral was brought to an end by their support of the Stuart cause during the risings of 1715 and 1745. For after the defeat of Charles Edward Stuart, 'The Young Pretender', part of the Hanoverian policy of ensuring the end of Stuart claims to the throne was to impose heavy fines on those who had been leading supporters of the Jacobite cause. By 1798 the mortgage debt on Balmoral had become too heavy and the estate was sold to James Duff, 2nd Earl of Fife.

Lord Fife never intended to live at Balmoral, but bought it as an investment for re-letting: he had both inherited and expanded enormous estates which contained more suitably grand houses, such as Duff House in Banff, built by Robert Adam. The second earl's estates were so extensive in Morayshire, Banffshire and Aberdeenshire that in the latter decades of the eighteenth century he was reputed to have controlled the political elections in all three counties. After a number of short lets the lease was taken in 1831 by Sir Robert Gordon, who thereby returned to the seat which his family had lost over a hundred and fifty years before. Sir Robert's affection for Balmoral and Deeside was such that he extended his

The meticulously kept kitchen garden and main conservatory. Behind, the prospect of towers and turrets rising out of deep woodland epitomizes the early Scottish romanticism conceived by Sir Walter Scott

original lease of five years for a further thirty-eight.

It is obvious that Sir Robert had intended to establish a home of comfort and enjoyment at Balmoral. In 1833 he made the deer forest, and in 1834 called in John Smith, an architect from Aberdeen, to make alterations to the house. 'Tudor Johnnie's' alterations completely transformed the old building, of which little was left recognizable except the seventeenth-century tower. The new additions included a conservatory – these were to become a widespread Victorian fashion. In Scotland their fashionable status was obviously enhanced by practical reasons, for within their protection a better quality and variety of plants could be grown without having to struggle against the late-spring and early-autumn frosts, and the frequently low temperatures.

On their arrival at Balmoral in 1848 Queen Victoria and Prince Albert's expectations were rapidly fulfilled. The house itself was perfectly adequate but, more important, the larger setting immediately captured their hearts. The wilderness of the surrounding wooded hills, broken by the winding course of the Dee valley, seemed to embody everything that they had found most appealing about Scotland. In 1842 Prince Albert's first impression of Perth was its similarity to the town of Basle, and there are constant comparisons in their journals and correspondence. Soon after their arrival in September Queen Victoria noted how the countryside bore an agreeable resemblance to the Thüringerwald; one of the strongest attractions of Scotland was always that it reminded Queen Victoria and her husband of Prince Albert's homeland in Germany.

Once securely established, Balmoral became Prince Albert's consuming passion for the few remaining years of his life. At Osborne he had already shown his zest for applying his planning mind to the business of making a home. But Balmoral was something different. Here he could work on a far more ambitious scale in a project for which his commitment was continually growing, building a new house, laying out the grounds and developing the estate. In the sadly short time allowed, his achievements and the devotion with which he pursued them, were such that Balmoral will always be indelibly stamped with their results. So highly did Queen Victoria esteem his qualities that his work received her continual encouragement and admiration. A strong foundation of their devoted marriage was her desire to channel her vivacity and wilfulness into her regard for him. 'Every year my heart becomes more fixed in this dear Paradise, and so much more so now, that *all* has become my dear Albert's *own* creation, own building, own laying out, as at *Osborne*; and his great taste, and the impress of his dear hand, have been stamped everywhere.'[7]

The years from 1848–52 were a frustrating period for Prince Albert as he was limited in his plans for Balmoral to making a few alterations to the old castle. But once the purchase was agreed work could begin in earnest; within days of arriving at Balmoral in the autumn of 1852 the Prince was discussing the building of a new castle with William Smith, the City

Architect for Aberdeen, whose father had rebuilt the old castle for Sir Robert Gordon. The old castle was not large enough for the Royal Family – there were now six children – and the large retinue of household staff and guests who were always in attendance. A site was chosen 100 yards to the north-west of the old castle, which not only afforded far better views of the surrounding countryside, particularly to the west and along the river, but also allowed for continued inhabitance of the old house while building was in progress.

The new Balmoral was built in a style widely thought to be in harmony with Highland scenery. Scottish baronial architecture was very popular in a country which was still enjoying a wave of Romanticism in its art and literature, largely due to the career and works of Sir Walter Scott. Scott had been a great admirer of King George IV and undoubtedly played a prominent part in the King's decision to visit Scotland in 1822. It is possible to see Queen Victoria and Prince Albert's awareness of Scott's influence in their attitude to the surroundings of Balmoral and the life they would live there. The appeal of the wild scenery, the turreted castle and the craze for tartans which became evident at Balmoral were all part of the romantic Scottish world Scott had created and which Queen Victoria, aided by Landseer, was later to develop into something intensely sentimental.

The prospect of towers and pointed turrets rising out of deep woodland, as at Balmoral, was totally in keeping with this mood; and for Prince Albert it had the equally compelling appeal of a Germanic flavour. In contrast to many castles of the same period which are somewhat brooding in appearance, the new Balmoral was given a freshness by the unusually white granite of which it was built. Prince Albert was determined to use local labour and local materials and as far as possible to make Balmoral part of the life of the local community. The granite came from quarries at Glen Gelder on the Balmoral estate, and the slate for the roof from the nearby Foundland quarries at Strathbogie.

As the new castle neared completion Prince Albert was able to turn his attention to laying out the surrounding grounds and gardens, which were to become such an essential part of the world Queen Victoria and he were creating for themselves, applying himself to the work with characteristic energy and attention to detail. James Forbes Beattie, a surveyor, was consulted for advice, as was James Giles, the artist who had done a series of sketches of Balmoral for Queen Victoria and Prince Albert when they were considering acquiring the castle in 1848. The basis of Prince Albert's plans was his model of the grounds, made in sand, in which the gardens, trees, paths and gates were positioned. Around the castle small formal gardens were laid out and filled with flower-beds in a manner typical of the day. Many of the flowers were roses and selected so that, as far as possible, they were in colourful bloom during the Royal Family's autumn visit. The main rose garden was beneath the west front of the castle where Queen

Victoria had her apartments, looking out on to the garden and beyond to a spectacular view down the Dee valley. In 1856, the day after arriving at Balmoral, Queen Victoria wrote in her journal: 'We walked along the river and outside the house. The new offices and the yard are excellent; and the little garden on the west side, with the eagle fountain which the King of Prussia gave me, and which used to be in the greenhouse at Windsor, is extremely pretty; as are also the flower-beds under the walls of the side which faces the Dee.'[8]

More important than the flower gardens in the development of

Opposite : The sheltered Tower Garden, partially enclosed by the east front and wing of the castle, and dominated by the clock tower.

The sunken rose garden, made by King George V and Queen Mary, below the west front of the castle. There has been a flower garden here since Queen Victoria and Prince Albert bought Balmoral. It was this view of Deeside which Queen Victoria looked out onto from her private apartments

Balmoral's surroundings were the trees that Prince Albert planted in the grounds. They were part of his desire for evocative reminders of the countryside of his youth, as well as being part of his plans for Balmoral to be enjoyed by future generations of Royal owners. The sight of the imposing specimen conifers on either side of the drive from the main gates to the castle cannot fail strongly to influence a person's first impressions of Balmoral; it is a true legacy of Prince Albert's work. Among the conifers are *Abies procera*, 'Noble Fir', which form an avenue along part of the main drive; *Abies grandis*, 'Giant Fir'; and *Tsuga albertiana*, 'Western Hemlock' – all trees which grow to an imposing stature. Also plentiful among the plantings were *Populus alba*, 'White Poplar', one of Prince Albert's favourite trees, grown from saplings sent from Coburg. As the trees grew up they helped to ensure the privacy of Balmoral which was so important to Queen Victoria and her husband, as well as giving the grounds of the castle a particular character which they have always retained.

In the short time before his death in 1861 Prince Albert achieved a great deal at Balmoral. It offered a practical outlet for his extremely active and intellectual mind, which all too often had to be content with committing its ideas and conclusions to his journal and letters. As well as the practicalities of developing the grounds and managing the estate, Prince Albert also showed in his work a determination to put into practise his philanthropic ideas. In his speeches as chairman of the Society for Improving the Condition of the Working Classes he showed a constant awareness of the problems of the poorer folks. At Balmoral he was able to provide employment for gardeners, keepers and estate workers, whose livelihoods could be helped by new cottages. Indeed, in the informality of much of their approach to life at Balmoral Queen Victoria and Prince Albert showed a new side of the monarchy. Away from the political frontiers of London and Windsor they were able actively to involve themselves with the people. Queen Victoria was often to be seen visiting the people of Crathie village in their cottages, and establishing links on a personal level.

As has often been recorded, Queen Victoria never recovered from the blow of her husband's death; and nowhere did she feel the loss more acutely than at Balmoral. Not only was it the home that they had discovered and come to love together, but all around was evidence of his work. As a result, she extended the time she spent there to include a visit in spring as well as autumn, and determined that as little as possible would be altered. It was at Balmoral, with memories of her husband so immediate and so numerous, that Queen Victoria felt most able to come to terms with the loneliness of her widowhood which was to last for forty years.

After the death of her husband Queen Victoria's expeditions from Balmoral became less frequent, and the gardens and grounds of the castle played a large part in her enjoyment of her visits. Queen Victoria's resolution to change as little as possible of her husband's work was absolute, and over the years the only additions were memorials and the new trees which Queen Victoria planted to record various events, happy or sad. The main addition was the statue of The Prince Consort by William Tweed which was placed looking over the road along the south bank of the Dee.

The secluded privacy of Queen Victoria's life at Balmoral was interrupted only by the daily business of state, which was very often dealt with in the Garden Cottage. Standing squat amongst protecting trees, the cottage was originally built by Prince Albert for the head gardener. But

after Prince Albert's death Queen Victoria began using it, and in 1895 she rebuilt it. Here she spent mornings dealing with her correspondence and state papers undisturbed, left alone to her work and her thoughts. In the days before the telephone and air travel Queen Victoria was always attended by a Minister of State, many of whom recorded their own impressions of Balmoral. During his stays when Prime Minister, Gladstone walked energetically for miles in the hills around Deeside. Disraeli, in contrast, was content to wander in the gardens of which he recorded his impressions on one occasion. 'An expanse of green and shaven lawn more extensive than that from the terrace at Clifden, and singularly striking in a land of mountains; but HM told me, that it was all artificial, and they had levelled a rugged and undulating soil. In short,

Queen Mary's Garden with, beyond, the regular lawns and borders of the lower garden

William Tweed's statue of
Prince Albert and the
Garden Cottage, originally
built by the Prince for the
head gardener and much
loved by Queen Victoria
after her husband's death

our garden at Hughenden on a great scale: except this was a broad green glade, the flower garden being at the other side of the castle.'

Queen Victoria's death in 1901 marked a watershed for Balmoral. Fifty-three years after the Prince Consort had initially acquired the estate it remained, and continued to be, steeped in an atmosphere of the past. On his accession King Edward VII inherited Balmoral, and he and Queen Alexandra moved there from Abergeldie Castle for their Scottish holidays. But for both Sandringham was always their favourite home, and the King limited his stays at Balmoral to one month a year or sometimes less. Queen Alexandra undoubtedly prefered Balmoral to Abergeldie, and the Duchess of York soon remarked how much more her mother-in-law was enjoying her Scottish holidays since moving there. Unlike Buckingham Palace and Windsor, Queen Alexandra determined to leave Queen Victoria's world at Balmoral as little altered as possible: from her correspondence it is clear that she felt Queen Victoria's influence on Balmoral very strongly. Sandringham was always to be the home of Edwardian society, and Balmoral remained a survivor from the previous era.

Edward VII's accession had meant that Abergeldie Castle became the Deeside home of the Prince and Princess of Wales, later King George V and Queen Mary, as it had been his when Queen Victoria was alive. The new Princess of Wales's first visit in August 1902, without her husband, who was at Cowes, did not start well. She was expecting her fifth child, the weather was appalling and any flowers or fruit in the walled garden had been ruined by the rain. Nor did the castle hold the fond family memories for her as it did for Prince George and his mother. However, things improved before the end of the visit, and the Princess recorded that she was able to go round the garden with the gardener, 'suggesting things for him to plant another year'. She also suggested that three old cherry trees should have climbers planted at the base to grow into their branches. During the next few years the gardens improved considerably, and by 1905 Princess May was able to write, 'The garden here is looking very pretty, but owing to the want of rain the sweet pea hedge is not as pretty as last year.'[9]

The interest which Princess May had shown in the gardens at Abergeldie was transferred to Balmoral when her husband inherited it on his accession in 1910. During her first visit to Balmoral after the First World War Queen Mary planted a single tree, a *Picea nobilis*, at the junction of the main drive and the road from Easter Balmoral. It is probable that her choice of tree was deliberately similar to many of those planted by Prince Albert because of a desire to perpetuate Balmoral's Victorian atmosphere. It is certain that part of King George V's growing love of Balmoral was in deference to his grandparents, knowing how special a part it had played in their lives. As Prince Albert had done before him, King George V took great interest in the estate and in the lives and livelihoods of its people. When not stalking or shooting he was happiest walking on his own, stopping to talk to people or visiting their cottages as it pleased him, with the manner of relaxed informality which characterized much of his life both at Balmoral and at Sandringham. For King George V and Queen Mary Balmoral became a home for regular autumn holidays in much the same way as it had for Queen Victoria and Prince Albert.

Both King George V and Queen Mary were products of the old order which was so radically altered by the events of 1914–18, and to such a large extent destroyed; they found themselves faced with the task of establishing the role of the monarchy in changed times. During the years immediately after the First World War Balmoral was a source of strength – its unbroken links with the past restored confidence in a world of uncertainty. At Balmoral George V was most conscious of the abiding influence of Queen Victoria. On 22 January 1924, the day that Ramsay MacDonald became the first Labour Prime Minister, he wrote in his diary, 'Today, twenty-three years ago, dear Grandmama died. I wonder what she would have thought of a Labour Government!' But, because of his unwavering sense of duty to his people, King George V was more ready to accept the changes of the post-war world than many of his subjects. A few weeks later in 1924 he wrote, 'They [the new Ministers] have different ideas from ours as they are all Socialists, but they ought to be given a chance and ought to be treated fairly.'[10] It was in this mood that the King entertained Ramsay MacDonald at Balmoral, where he did so much to establish the relationship of respect and friendliness which came to exist between the two men.

In a letter to Queen Mary written on 24 August 1924 King George V said, 'I am sure you will like the new alterations in our garden here, the wall of rocks with flowers is a great success and I congratulated Mrs Ramsay and Chalmers on their labours.'[11] (Mrs Ramsay was the wife

of Captain (later Sir) J. D. Ramsay, the Commissioner at Balmoral; and Chalmers was the head gardener.) The 'new alterations' comprised a small garden that came to be known as Queen Mary's Garden, situated beyond the main lawn on the south side of the castle. In character with the existing ones around the castle, the garden was simple in design, with a low semi-circular wall of rocks planted with alpines leading to a fountain, around which were planted small flower-beds. The wall was broken by a flight of steps and a pair of wrought iron gates with the monograms 'GR' and 'MR'. These gates were put up in 1923, at the same time as the main entrance gates bearing the same monograms; both pairs were made by the local blacksmith.

A year later, in 1925, King George V was able to write and tell his wife of another development in the gardens, 'The new sunk garden in front of our windows is a great success and I am sure you will like it as much as I do ... [it] is full of flowers; I congratulated Lady Ramsay, she has worked very hard with Chalmers (who of course I have not seen yet) to get it finished in time.'[12] The sunken garden was added beyond the existing rose garden on the west side of the castle, and filled with formally laid out beds of roses.

King George V died in 1936. Despite the changes during his lifetime which had directly affected him and his position, Queen Mary and he had, at Balmoral, been able to perpetuate traditions at the same time as leaving reminders of their presence and affection for the place. The few months of King Edward VIII's reign gave him little time to visit Balmoral, although he caused something of a stir in the family when, during a visit, Mrs Simpson was a guest, and ostensibly acted as his hostess. After his abdication in 1936 Balmoral once again became a family holiday home for King George VI, Queen Elizabeth and their two young daughters, providing at least some respite from the growing tension in Europe. A story is told of one incident which must have provided some light-hearted relief: in 1938, shortly before leaving for the Munich conference, Neville Chamberlain was at Balmoral and it was suggested that the Princesses Elizabeth and Margaret show him round the gardens. The Prime Minister was later discovered sliding down a steep grass terrace on a tea-tray, helplessly out of control, much to the glee of the young Princesses, for whom 'tobogganing' was a favourite pastime.

King George VI and Queen Elizabeth had already shown their love of gardens, and indeed of active gardening, at the Royal Lodge. At Balmoral they were happy to enjoy the gardens as they found them, and it very quickly became a well-loved home, not least because of Queen Elizabeth's fond memories of her own Scottish childhood at Glamis. One of King George VI's favourite areas was the formal pansy garden which lay below the ballroom terrace. These beds had probably been laid out during King George V and Queen Mary's time, and provided an intricate carpet of colour below the windows of the house. During Queen Elizabeth II's reign

Opposite: The lower garden, with early morning mist lingering on the steep wooded hillside behind

there have been changes in the gardens at Balmoral, but none which detract from their traditional nature; and it would no doubt delight Queen Victoria and Prince Albert to know that in essence Balmoral is still largely as they created it over a hundred years ago. One important link with the days of Prince Albert has been the continuing interest of the Royal Family in the maintenance of an efficient and modern estate. Forestry plays a major part in its economics and when, in 1953, gales destroyed hundreds of trees in plantations laid out by Prince Albert they were faithfully replanted. In other places where the trees have reached maturity they have been felled and replanted. One sad loss in 1965 was the sale of the Ayrshire dairy herd which rendered obsolete the dairy designed by Prince Albert in the 1850s. The fact that the building had functioned efficiently for over a hundred years is a reflection on its far-sighted planning and quality.

In the grounds of the castle many of the trees have also reached maturity, and on either side of the main lawn conifers blend with the softer canopies of beech and copper beech. Their size makes the open greenness of the lawn even more striking than it must have been when Disraeli remarked upon it, and it is surely this quintessential view of the castle which makes the most lasting impression. At the far end of the lawn are the gates to Queen Mary's Garden; this has been extended till today it makes up the major part of the gardens. The central path leads past the fountain to a second walled terrace beyond which a lower lawn is enclosed by mixed herbaceous borders. Between the central borders a *Prunus avium*, 'Wild Cherry', which is over sixty years old used to stand alone, but now has a copper-leaf acer as companion. It was the Duke of Edinburgh's suggestion to back the two long borders flanking this lower garden with hedges of *Chamaecyparis lawsoniana*, which have grown rapidly since they were planted in the 1950s. The enclosed atmosphere they give to the garden is accentuated by the backcloth of the hill rising up behind.

To one side of the lower garden is the kitchen garden, which was moved in the 1950s from its position near the East Lodge between the castle and Easter Balmoral. The path to the kitchen garden passes the conservatory which during the weeks of the Royal Family's autumn visit is filled with a brilliant display of plants – fuschias, pelargoniums, begonias, celosias, gloxinias and many others. Across Queen Mary's Garden a path leads out under a metal arbour, in August heavy with the scent of its honeysuckle to Queen Victoria's Garden Cottage.

Beyond the Garden Cottage lies the most recent addition to the grounds of Balmoral, the Water Garden, devised by the Duke of Edinburgh. Here a semi-woodland state is preserved and soon the pond will be enticingly screened by young trees and shrubs – birch, acers and rhododendrons – which are growing up in the shelter of mature conifers. Although their contents have changed over the years, the gardens around the castle itself, sheltering under its walls, have altered little in form since the days of Queen Victoria and Prince Albert. Beside the front door is a narrow border of nasturtiums out of which a *Traphellium* grows trained against the wall. Better known as the 'Scotch flame flower', its name derives from its delicate but brilliant red flowers. Close by, also on the main south front of the castle, is the Tower Garden. Its lawn, surrounded by borders of *Fuchsia riccartonii*, buddleias and ampelopsis, is enclosed on two sides and has the sheltered atmosphere of a courtyard. The stillness is broken only by the Cherub Fountain which plays in the centre.

The windows of the west front of the castle, where Queen Victoria had her apartments, have always commanded the most striking views of the countryside stretching away down the wooded valley of the River Dee. Here one can appreciate how the gardens enhance the views from the castle. In the immediate foreground is the brilliant colour of the rose garden planned, like the other gardens, to be in flower during the Royal Family's autumn visit. The pink of the 'Betty Prior' polyantha rose in the borders around the Chamois statue, and the kaleidoscope of mixed floribunda roses in the sunken garden, add warmth to the white of the castle walls and offset the openness beyond. Around the sunken borders the stone walls are given colour by small alpines and white mallow.

The flight of balustraded granite steps which descends from the rose garden to the lawn in front of the ballroom has been the scene of many Royal photographs in the past, including, in 1896, a group with Tzar Nicholas II and his wife during their only visit to Balmoral. The pansy garden which King George VI was so fond of has disappeared, possibly necessitated by a reduction in the number of gardeners, but beyond the present lawn is the relatively new ballroom border, planted in 1968, whose shrub roses, herbaceous and annual plants set off the young silver birch, acers and rhododendrons by the banks of the Dee. Although hidden from view the sounds of the river can be caught on the breeze, conveying its timeless and tranquil presence. The views up and down stream from the riverbank are quite spectacular, and as much as anything typify the beauty of Balmoral which first captured Queen Victoria and which has remained unchanged to the present day.

BIRKHALL

Aberdeenshire

BIRKHALL AND ITS ESTATE of 6500 acres was the first property on Deeside to come into the ownership of the Royal Family and, although relatively little-known, the charming and unpretentious house has always played a very special part in their autumn visits to Scotland. Prince Albert bought the property from the Gordon family in 1849, the same Gordons with whom he had negotiated over Balmoral and Abergeldie. Birkhall itself was bought in the Prince of Wales's name, who was then eight years old; Prince Albert, planning ahead with characteristic thoroughness, envisaged it as an ideal Scottish residence for his eldest son. In fact the Prince of Wales stayed there only once, in 1862; after his marriage a year later Princess Alexandra and he preferred to stay at Abergeldie when they were in Scotland. However, Birkhall has been visited by various members of the Royal Family since then and is now the Deeside home of the Queen Mother. Its role could be described as the Dower House of Balmoral, for although the two properties have always been linked, the eight miles between them, and Birkhall's remote position on Glen Muick, give the little house a distinct air of detachment.

Birkhall had been associated with Abergeldie, with whose lands it marches, since 1449 when King James II (of Scotland) granted the barony of Abergeldie to Alexander Seton, Lord Gordon, who was created Earl of Huntly. The barony included Birkhall, which was then known as Stiren from the Gaelic word *stairean*, meaning stepping-stones (there was a ford with stepping-stones across the River Muick close by). Huntly's son, Sir Alexander Gordon, who inherited the property also became the first Gordon laird of Abergeldie, so for the next two hundred and fifty years Birkhall was effectively part of the Abergeldie estate. But in 1698 Rachel Gordon succeeded her brother as

Opposite : The central path of the lower garden, aligned with the original part of the house. The Queen Mother's new L-shaped wing extends to the left.

The 'chain bridge' described by Princess Alice, Countess of Athlone as: 'heavenly to jump upon, which spanned the rushing little Muick where we loved to play'

Right: The yew 'doorway' leads to the garden nearest the house

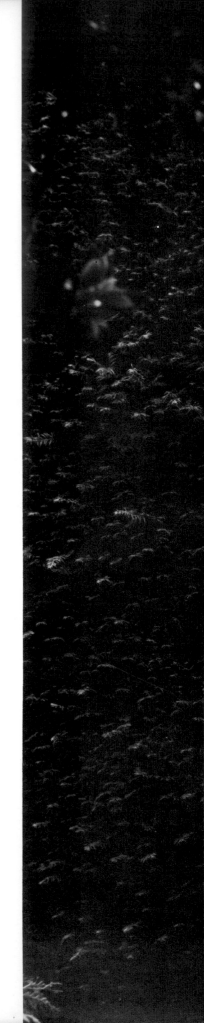

the tenth laird, and married Captain Charles Gordon. It was they who, in 1715, built the original portion of the present house which became the home of Joseph, the youngest of their three sons. It is ironic that a house which, during the first half of the eighteenth century, was a hot-bed of Jacobite fervour, should now be in the possession of the Royal Family. Charles Gordon had supported the 1715 rising and his youngest son Joseph took part in that of 1745, forced into hiding near Birkhall after the Battle of Culloden. His wife Elizabeth was an equally fervent Jacobite and it was she who arranged the escape of the Oliphants of Gask to Sweden after hiding tham at Birkhall.

The construction of the new house was commemorated by the inscription over the old entrance: *17. C.G. R.G. 15*. It was a typical example of the Scottish 'Ha-House', a style which, by the 1700s, was beginning to replace the castellated buildings of previous centuries. Built of granite and roofed with slates from the local quarry of Meall Dudn, the house was a simple rectangular building with a basement, two storeys and an attic. Birkhall's main appeal lies in its setting, overlooking the River Muick rushing past towards Ballater where it joins the River Dee, with Glen Muick stretching away behind towards the high and lonely Loch Muick at the river's head.

The gardens on to which the east front of the house looks have probably not changed much in shape since the early eighteenth century: the lawns in front of the house lead to the steep terracing above the bowl-shaped lower garden; beyond stretch the tree-lined banks of the River Muick. There would have been flowers, fruit and vegetables planted together in a typically Scottish manner, as they are now, giving the gardens a cheerful, thriving appearance. The chief limitation in choice of plants has always been the sharp frosts which descend into the basin of the garden; as a result late summer and autumn provide the best displays here.

For some years after Birkhall's rejection by the Prince of Wales in 1863, it was normally occupied during the Royal visits to Balmoral by a member of Queen Victoria's Household. A regular tenant was Sir James Clark, the Queen's physician, whose advice had led to the original purchase of Balmoral. Although Queen Victoria did not stay at Birkhall she greatly enjoyed visiting the house and its secluded little garden. One can imagine her driving from Balmoral to take tea there, in much the same way as she used to visit Frogmore and the Royal Lodge from Windsor Castle. In 1856 Queen Victoria invited Florence Nightingale to stay at Birkhall as her guest. The Queen visited her daily, and together they walked in the garden discussing plans for an army medical service, the need for which had become painfully obvious during the Crimean War. Lord Panmure, the Secretary of State for War, was summoned to Balmoral, and, thanks largely to the two determined women, plans were put in motion for the foundation of the Royal Army Medical Corps.

Another reason for Queen Victoria's affection for Birkhall was its position on the road to some of her favourite haunts. First in importance of these was the 'shiel' or cottage, called Alt-na-Giuthasach, near the eastern end of Loch Muick, which she and Prince Albert visited regularly from 1849 until his death in 1861. After Prince Albert's death Queen Victoria felt unable to continue using Alt-na-Giuthasach, so full of vivid memories of her husband. Instead she built herself another shiel, Glassalt Shiel, in an even more remote position at the bleak and lonely western end of Loch Muick. Some of Queen Victoria's staff deplored her visits to 'The Widow's House' as she called it, for she would often be away, totally out of touch, for days on end. But its solitude helped the Queen come to terms with the unhappiness of her widowhood. During her visits to Balmoral after the Prince Consort's death Queen Victoria's search for

Looking from the garden to the River Muick below and, beyond, the wooded hills of Glen Muick which surround Birkhall

privacy and peace almost overrode other concerns; and in that search she constantly sought strength in the rugged countryside behind Birkhall which led up Glen Muick.

By 1885 it was abundantly clear to Queen Victoria that the Prince of Wales did not wish to use Birkhall when he was in Scotland and she was worried that being inhabited only on an occasional basis by members of her Household, the house was not being cared for as she would have liked. Therefore in that year the Queen purchased Birkhall from her son and in so doing had the satisfaction of knowing that she possessed, save the Abergeldie estates, all the land from Birkhall to the Invercauld bridge, upstream from Balmoral, and most of the Forest of Ballochbuie which lay up the Dee between Balmoral and Braemar.

In 1884, a year before Queen Victoria bought Birkhall from the Prince of Wales, her youngest son, Prince Leopold, had died very suddenly at the early age of thirty-one. He left a young widow, Princess Helen, Duchess of Albany, and their two children: Princess Alice (who later married the Earl of Athlone) and Prince Charles Edward (who succeeded his uncle as Duke of Saxe-Coburg and Gotha in 1900). During the later years of the nineteenth century the Duchess of Albany and her children stayed at Birkhall on a number of occasions at the invitation of Queen Victoria. In her memoirs *For My Grandchildren* Princess Alice, Countess of Athlone, recalled these visits; one passage illustrates the degree of continuity in the gardens' present appearance. 'Here we spent some of the happiest days of our lives. It was a small place in those days. We loved the sloping garden full of fruit and sweet peas and, at the bottom, a chain bridge, heavenly to jump upon, which spanned the rushing little Muick where we loved to play.'

After Queen Victoria's death Birkhall continued to be used by various members of the Royal Family or members of King Edward VII's Household, although the King's visits to Scotland were far less regular than his mother's had been. It is possible that Sir Dighton Probyn, who had become the King's Keeper of the Privy Purse, stayed at Birkhall and made one or two alterations to the gardens. But it was not until after the First World War, during King George V's reign, that Birkhall came into its own as a regular residence of the immediate Royal Family. The King offered the house to his sons the Prince of Wales (later King Edward VIII), the Duke of York (later King George VI), the Duke of Gloucester and the Duke of Kent. For the Duke of York and his young Duchess (formerly Lady Elizabeth Bowes-Lyon) whom he had married in 1923, Birkhall became, as it had been for Princess Alice's family, a favourite holiday home.

After their marriage, and particularly after the births of their two daughters, Princess Elizabeth in 1926 and Princess Margaret in 1930, the Duke and Duchess of York were always relieved to be able to mix their official life with a quiet private family life, for which Birkhall – like the

Royal Lodge – was well suited. The Duke of York's love of shooting made their visits to Scotland especially enjoyable; the Duchess's favourite sporting activity was fly-fishing (at which she has long been expert). Birkhall presented ample opportunities for both these pastimes. As might be expected, it was not long before the Duke and Duchess began making plans for the garden at Birkhall as they were doing, in a far more ambitious manner, at the Royal Lodge. The Birkhall garden always appealed especially to the Duchess of York, who loved its homely, informal nature and was intrigued by its unusual shape.

When the Yorks left London for Birkhall in the autumn of 1936 the new King Edward VIII was on his notorious cruise of the eastern Mediterranean aboard the yacht *Nahlin*; the crisis of the abdication was moving steadily towards its climax. On 10 December that year Edward VIII signed the instrument of his abdication. The Archbishop of Canterbury, Cosmo Lang, was staying with the Yorks at Birkhall. Despite the evident tension he wrote afterwards: 'A delightful visit. They were kindness itself. The old house is full of charm, and the Duchess has done much with the garden. Strange to think of the destiny which may be awaiting the little Elizabeth, at present second from the throne.'

King George VI's accession in 1936 brought to an end the family's visits to Birkhall, since Balmoral was the official residence for their autumn visits to Scotland. But even in the relatively few years they stayed at Birkhall the Duke and Duchess of York had left their mark on the garden. It was the Duchess's passion for colour and flowers wherever possible which provided the most striking additions. Surrounding the rows of vegetables and fruit on either side of the central path in the lower garden were borders thick with Michaelmas daisies and bright trimmings of white heather. The two herbaceous borders were filled with autumn plants. Outstanding in the shorter of the two borders was the clump of giant *Cardiocrinum* (*Lilium*) *giganteum*, whose successful cultivation was something of a triumph and reflected the rich moistness of the soil at Birkhall. It seemed that every possible area was cultivated in some form, even the steep slopes of the long terrace were planted with rows of various flowers and vegetables.

The premature death of King George VI in 1952 brought the return of Queen Elizabeth to Birkhall, for her daughter offered her the use of the house whenever she was staying on Deeside. Although the Queen Mother was soon to acquire a new Scottish home of her own, the Castle of Mey, she has continued to give Birkhall the loving and energetic attention which all her homes, however temporary, have received. Shortly after her return there she determined to replace the wing on the south end of the house, by all accounts a somewhat rough-and-ready affair with a corrugated iron roof and a large ivy plant spreading its tentacles through the drawing room inside, with a new one. It was to be L-shaped and would, with a first floor, greatly expand the accommodation for guests.

Painted white and roofed with the grey slates, the new wing blends so effectively with the old house that it is not easy to realize the two hundred and forty year age-difference. Typical of her thoughtful planning, the new French doors are so aligned that they provide a direct view through the wrought-iron gate on the tall hedge of *Chamaecyparis lawsoniana*, stretching from the corner of the old house along the north side of the main lawn, to the spire of Ballater church in the distance.

The Queen Mother brought new life to the reposeful 'dower house' atmosphere of Birkhall. The house was filled with guests for shooting parties or fishing expeditions, and the days were regularly punctuated by visits from The Queen, the Duke of Edinburgh and their children, as well as from other members of the Royal Family and friends staying along the valley at Balmoral. Plans for the garden were an automatic part of the general activity. Lord Adam Gordon, who was Comptroller of the Queen Mother's Household from 1953 to 1973 and himself a keen and expert gardener, clearly remembers collecting for the Queen Mother – and often with her – heathers, alpines and in particular gentians, for a curving rock garden on the sloping ground to the south of the new wing. Close to the rock garden was a stand of apple trees which the Queen Mother had planted with King George VI during one of their stays at Birkhall in the 1930s. The Queen Mother has steadily added to the collection of miniature plants, one of her main delights in the Birkhall garden, and often makes a personal responsibility of the weeding during her stays.

It is inconceivable that one of the Queen Mother's gardens should not contain roses, one of her favourite flowers, and in recent years a rose garden has made its appearance at Birkhall. Flowering late because of the delayed Scottish summer, the blooms are often at their best during the Queen Mother's autumn visit, in particular the climbing 'Albertine' and 'New Dawn' roses trained against the east-facing garden front of the house. The Queen Mother has also planted a number of her favourite shrub roses on the slope beyond the new wing, leading up to the little summer-house at the top of the rising ground. The old borders flanking the central path in the lower part of the garden have been replaced with deep beds of Windsor phlox, which produce a spectacular mass of pink flowers. In the centre of the lower garden the path circles around a dome of clipped yew, and nearer to the river it passes through a 'doorway' of two tall clumps of similarly clipped yew. The yews – of some considerable age – are one of the garden's most interesting features, and from the bottom of the garden the narrow doorway, framing the central dome, provides a most effective introduction to the rows of colour, the steep terrace, and lawn rising to the house, which all lie beyond.

Enclosing this basin of bright colour and productivity are the two herbaceous borders; replenished once every three years and filled with large groups of plants such as phlox, Michaelmas daisies and dahlias. One

From the herbaceous border a path leads up the terrace, where part of one of the Queen Mother's monograms of marigolds is visible, and past the rockery to one of the summer houses perched overlooking the garden.

change the Queen Mother has made is to remove the rows of plants which used to climb the terrace up to the main lawn, and to lay down the long bank to grass. Six years ago gloss marigolds were planted in tight clusters to form two groups of her monogram 'ER', breaking up the long swathe of green.

Autumn may be the best time of year for the Birkhall garden but in the past the Queen Mother has, when possible, made visits earlier in the year, particularly for the spring fishing on the River Dee. As a result the gardens also contain a number of early flowers; the borders along the garden front of the house, below the climbing roses, are filled with spring wallflowers and hundreds of tulips, and the slopes beside the rock garden are carpeted with daffodils, a perfect foil for a stand of young Mediterranean oaks. Thus, for much of the year, the garden, with its shape determined by the eccentric contours of the ground, compliments the house and adds a note of sparkle without which the house, encircled as it is by the large Deeside scenery, would look somewhat overpowered by its surroundings.

The lawn in front of the house leads to the steep terrace, bordered with phlox, and to the main garden below

CASTLE OF MEY

Caithness

THE CASTLE OF MEY is the most unusual, the most romantic and the most personal of the Royal homes and when the Queen Mother first saw the castle in 1952 the possibility of buying it became irresistible. The Queen Mother explained part of her ambition when she later received the Freedom of Wick: 'I found The Castle of Mey, with its long history, its serene beauty and its proud setting, faced with the prospect of having no one to occupy it. I felt a great wish to preserve, if I could, this ancient dwelling. It is too common an experience to find that once a house becomes deserted its decay begins and it is a happiness to me to feel that I have been able to save from such a fate part of Scotland's heritage.' But as well as this were her own reasons which stemmed from closely guarded thoughts and feelings: the sense of loss and emptiness after the death of King George VI a few months earlier; the fact that she had left most of the homes she had shared with him and only retained others by the wish of The Queen. All this gave the Queen Mother a longing for somewhere she could really call her own. A new home would be a new interest which would give her strength to look forward to re-building her life after widowhood at the early age of fifty-one; and it was natural that she should look to Scotland.

The remoteness of the Castle of Mey immediately appealed to the Queen Mother in the way that Glassalt Shiel, isolated at the western end of Loch Muick high up behind Deeside, had appealed to Queen Victoria. The remoteness had a beauty of its own; when she first saw the Castle of Mey the Queen Mother must have had similar thoughts to Evelyn Burnaby who described travelling through Caithness in the 1880s: 'We could see no sign of habitation until at last, on suddenly descending by a

Opposite: Castle of Mey; the elevated view from the little garden tower shows how the old hedges divide up the walled garden into compartments; beyond, the west front of the castle

Overleaf: Mey, the most northerly castle in Britain

steep road, we caught a magnificent view, all in a moment, of Stroma Island, with the whole range of the Orkneys perfectly distinct.' As well as beauty there was romanticism: a little castle perched on the northernmost outpost of Britain's mainland, as it had been for four centuries. And on first sight the Castle of Mey was a challenge which could only have appealed to a spirit as adventurous, even wilful, as the Queen Mother's: derelict, with its gardens in decay and most of the surrounding land sold. The Queen Mother's achievement, against considerable odds, has proved an unqualified success and the castle is restored to the status it had enjoyed in the past.

The Castle of Mey was for centuries the family home of the Sinclairs of Mey, descended from George Sinclair, third and youngest son of the 4th Earl of Caithness (a title bestowed upon William Sinclair by King James II of Scotland in 1455). It was the 4th Earl, also George Sinclair, who built the castle, between 1566 when the Mey lands were acquired and 1572 when he granted them to his second son William. (In good Scottish tradition of the time William was strangled by his older brother John who was imprisoned until his death as a result, and thus the inheritance passed to George, the Earl's youngest son.) The castle was typical of many sixteenth- and seventeenth-century Scottish castles, built on the 'Z' plan with corbelled turrets. What made it distinctive was its pink-hued Caithness stone of marked difference from the forbidding grey walls of many Scottish castles. Its construction is recorded in a carving containing the Caithness and Montrose arms, as well as the initials 'G.S.' and 'E.G.' and the date 1566. The initials are those of George Sinclair, 4th Earl of Caithness, and his wife Elizabeth Graham, daughter of the Earl of Montrose. It is likely that the Earl did not complete the castle, and that it was left to his son George to finish the building between his father's death in 1582 and his own in 1616.

Eighteenth-century Caithness enjoyed considerable prosperity, largely through a thriving grain trade, and the character of the Caithness gentry, like the physical appearance of the county, clearly distinguished them from most of their fellow Highlanders. Staunch Episcopals, they supported the Anglican Church in clear preference to the Scottish Presbyterian Church. The common language was English, and they do not appear to have been beset with the problems of clan feuds as was the rest of the Highlands. All this, along with geographical remoteness, bred a social élitism manifested in great pride in their clothes, their food and wine, an interest in literature and a cultured life in general, and continual hospitality. Hand-in-hand with this good living went the hard living of heavy drinking and gambling, the downfall of many of the Caithness lairds. The existence of the Castle of Mey at all, or more correctly Barrogill Castle, as it was then called, was dependant upon the Sinclair's fortunes, which were continually fluctuating as a result of their extravagant lifestyle. In a period of eighteen months during the 1850s Sir James

Sinclair, who died virtually penniless, consumed with his friends and guests at Barrogill Castle 956 bottles of claret.

Sir James Sinclair may have died penniless but he did manage to restore the castle greatly after he had regained the estate in 1734 from Sir Patrick Dunbar of Bowermadden, who had seized it from his father (also Sir James) in lieu of considerable debts. In 1735 Bayne had written after a visit to Barrogill Castle: 'This fine lodging encloses a spacious area, in a quadrangle forme, the body of the principall lodging composes the first side, where besides a great number of large and very well furnished rooms, there's a spacious gallery of 50 feet long ceiled with wainscot carved out in curious figures. The other sides were once finely accommodated with upper rooms and below them officers' houses. But now the whole is very much decayed and defaced and far short of its ancient splendour and magnificence.' But in the 1750s Sir James Sinclair spent two hundred pounds repairing the castle, and in 1762 Bishop Robert Forbes visited the castle and wrote: 'It is one of the best houses in all Caithness, consisting of about eighteen fine rooms, two of which being large dining rooms or halls, and one of these almost a cube.' Of equal relevance here was the Bishop's admiration of the very fine gardens growing apples, strawberries and cherries. In the same year Sir James placed a stone carving of the Sinclair arms over the north entrance to the courtyard of the castle, to celebrate its restoration.

Bishop Forbes's comments on the gardens are among the first to be found, although it is likely that the two-acre walled garden (still intact today) pre-dated the eighteenth century. Despite the relative warmth, provided by the Gulf Stream flowing through the Pentland Firth, which allows the growth of plants such as strawberries and cherries so far north, the overriding problem was and is the need for protection from the continual wind and rain sweeping across Caithness's flat landscape. The general conditions, even with walls, were such as precluded the cultivation of any plant which could not tolerate this continual battery.

Trouble continued for the Sinclairs until 1790, when Sir James's grandson of the same name inherited the family title and became 12th Earl of Caithness. He paid off the debts run up in the now familiar style by his father, and set about improving the Mey estates as a whole. He planted a great many trees among which may have been the sycamores flanking the present drive and standing to the east of the castle. The Earldom of Caithness remained with the Sinclairs of Mey for the next three generations, and it was during the tenure of James, the 14th Earl, that Mey appears to have enjoyed its first visit by members of the English Royal Family, the Prince and Princess of Wales (later King Edward VII and Queen Alexandra). In his book *The County of Caithness* John Horne records that the Prince and Princess visited John O'Groat's in 1876, accompanied by Prince John of Glucksburg. But a more likely date for the visit would appear to have been 1868, for in the gardens of the Castle of

Mey, standing beside the main entrance to the south of the castle, are an ash and a chestnut tree with plaques commemorating their planting in that year by the Prince and Princess of Wales respectively.

It was on the death of George Sinclair, 15th Earl of Caithness, that Barrogill Castle and the Mey estates ceased to belong to the Sinclairs. He died unmarried in 1899 – over three hundred years after his ancestor, the 4th Earl, had begun building the castle – and while the Earldom passed to a kinsman, James Sinclair, he bequeathed the estates to a friend, Mr Heathcote. They passed through two subsequent owners to Captain F. B. Inbert-Terry, and it was he who decided, in 1952, by which time the castle had been empty for some little while, to sell both the castle and the land, divided up into lots. It seemed then that the castle was irrevocably doomed.

In June 1952, four months after the death of King George VI, the Queen Mother had been staying with Commander and Lady Doris Vyner at their home near Dunnet, which rejoices in the fairy-tale name of The House of the Northern Gate. Lady Doris suggested a picnic expedition to the old deserted castle at Mey, which they had heard was up for sale. Picnicking has always been one of the Queen Mother's favourite pastimes – and one in which she indulges compulsively, whatever the weather and regardless of complaints from any less-enthusiastic companions. Perhaps the castle drive, lined and enclosed by sycamore trees, reminded her of the avenue leading to her old home at Glamis. There was the terrible thought that it might fall into ruin beyond repair, and no doubt the Queen Mother had a host of ideas of what she could make of the walled garden. She left not only captivated but determined to buy the castle. By doing so she would not only secure its future but put a new light into her own.

At its sale the castle was described as having: 'all the external dignity of an ancient Highland residence'. But in 1952 the description of another previous owner was more apposite: gaunt and windswept, shabby and neglected. In fact, the castle was fast becoming a shell, and the garden area, including the walled garden to the west, was totally neglected. But the Queen Mother would not be deterred; in August 1952 – after a number of other, surreptitious, visits to The House of the Northern Gate – she put in a successful bid and the property – castle, garden and a small area of farmland – became hers.

It seemed that the Castle of Mey – the Queen Mother's first decision was to restore its ancient name – was dogged by bad luck, for severe storms during the winter of 1952–3 removed virtually all that remained of the roof. The renovation of the castle took three long years, but in the autumn of 1955 the Queen Mother was able to stay in her new home for the first time and proudly fly her personal standard from the flagstaff. In a charming way, and by searching exhaustively for exactly the right pieces of furniture, paintings and other decorations, the Queen Mother succeeded in blending her own personal taste with the traditional character of the

Previous page: Sunlight breaking through the dense branches of sycamore to ferns and primulas thriving in the damp soil

One of the narrow paths enclosed by the old hedges and flower borders of the walled garden

Overleaf: The walled garden; behind, the exposed and flattened canopy of the sycamore trees

castle. Her search included tracking down a number of the Sinclair family possessions, which came to light in local antique shops and beyond.

Because the castle was so completely off the beaten track, privacy and informality – the former carefully safeguarded at other Royal homes but the latter often impossible – were totally natural and reassuringly secure. Members of the Queen Mother's Household say that, without doubt, the Castle of Mey is where the Queen Mother is most relaxed and possibly most contented. For a few weeks each year her life there is completely her own.

A neglected garden is as sad a sight as a neglected house, especially to the Queen Mother for whom gardens are so precious. She was helped by being able to build around those parts of the garden which had survived, in particular the protective walls which are the basis of its existence. From

the seaward front of the castle an unbroken line of stone wall stretches from the east side to join the main east tower, and from the west side to join the lower wall of the walled garden, in the far corner of which is an enchanting castellated tower.

In the walled garden there remained one of the garden's outstanding features, the old hedges which divide the area into a series of protected

The unexpected richness of growth at Mey is visible in the mixed border beyond the rose garden

squares, with narrow paths running around the perimeter of each and at right-angles through the middle. The hedges are made up of a most unusual mixture of bushes: mainly hardy fuchsia, elder and hawthorn, with privet, wild dog-roses and flowering currants scattered about. It is the relative mildness of Mey's climate which allows the hardy fuchsias to survive not only in the hedges but as large shrubs in other parts of the garden. Other welcome survivors in the walled garden were the apple trees trained on the walls, and, best of all, the gigantic *Senecio greyi* trained against the south-facing wall. The small-scale, enclosed nature of the walled garden give it the atmosphere of a maze as the hedges continually hide what lies beyond until, on rounding a corner, or reaching the end of a path, another part of the pattern is revealed. Its mixture of vegetables, fruit and flowers – vegetables and fruit filling the central compartments and flowers in borders beneath the walls – is reminiscent of the garden at Birkhall, and in both the Queen Mother has succeeded in enhancing their traditional Scottish natures.

Two of the most important factors in the Queen Mother's additions to the walled garden have been variety and colour, particularly evident below the seaward, south-facing wall. In front of the *Senecio* existing hardy fuchsias and buddleias have been incorporated into a mixed border with potentilla, white chrysanthemums, antirrhinums, roses and gorgeous yellow *Primula florindae*. The primulas, with their tall slender stalks and golden crowns thrive throughout the garden and were all planted by the Queen Mother. Revelling in the perpetually damp and often saturated soil they fill a long border beside the path along the north side of the walled garden, on the other side from the mixed border, and are also planted in a deep border below the west wall. Beyond the mixed border a small fence swathed luxuriantly in honeysuckle hides what is perhaps the Queen Mother's favourite creation: the rose garden, which is almost miniature in size but perfectly proportioned. The formally laid out beds are filled with All Gold, Iceberg, Europeana and Glenfiddich and divided by paths of shells collected from the beaches around Mey. As a backcloth a nasturtium border, and Albertine roses and Clematis climbing the wall complete a picture which, perhaps best of all, illustrates the Queen Mother's influence on the garden.

The most spectacular display of colour is given by the little conservatory beyond the rose garden which, during the Queen Mother's visits, is filled with a kaleidoscopic mixture of begonias, fuchsias and geraniums. Not only do they make a fine display but they also meet one of the Queen Mother's requirements of any garden – to provide plants and flowers to fill her rooms. More subdued than the conservatory, rose garden and mixed border, but equally imaginative, is the herb garden below the north-facing wall; it contains every known common herb and even there colour is not lacking, for close by are sweet peas whose flowers look almost too delicate for Mey's demanding conditions.

Primula florindae, one of the garden's outstanding features, stretch towards the light beneath the sycamores to the east of the castle

Between the walled garden and the castle is an area enclosed on two sides by walls and on a third by the west front of the castle. It is one of the Queen Mother's favourite places for taking meals out of doors, or just to enjoy the peace. The wide lawn surrounded by roses – Albertines spreading all over the walls and Iceberg, Silver Jubilee and All Gold in borders – could have been transported from a more protected garden in southern England – where the croquet which is played might seem more at home. The view through the pair of gates in the north wall, over land sloping gently down to the Pentland Firth and beyond where the Orkneys, with the rock stack 'The Old Man of Hoy', occasionally break into sight through the mist, upholds Sir George Sitwell's belief that fundamental to a garden's character is the nature of and its relationship with the surrounding landscape.

The eastern front of the castle is dominated by the tall, narrow main tower and the long border stretching away along the east wall. Here are more large hardy fuchsias as well as a most unusual plant which for some time was a source of baffllement; a *Centaurea macrocephala*, 'Great Golden Knapweed', it originates from the Caucasus and was introduced into Britain in the early nineteenth century; its vibrant yellow flowers are shaped like those of a giant thistle. A path runs along the border and, rather eccentrically, leads nowhere except to the edge of the garden with glimpses into the intertwined branches of the sycamore wood beyond. Across it there is a host of primulas flattened by the continual wind, stretching their slender stems and clusters of golden flowers upward towards the umbrella-like canopy of sycamores. Only thin beams of sunlight filter through to catch their bright yellow; the effect is most mysterious and the

grotto-like atmosphere is strengthened by the rough beard of lychen clinging to the trees.

The appearance of the sycamores is nowhere more striking than along the main drive which, as it nears the castle, becomes a trellised avenue whose trees have submitted to the continual battering of the wind and crouch, bent and twisted. In contrast to their gauntness a thick yellow carpet of celendines greets the Queen Mother when she visits Mey in the spring.

During the last twenty-nine years the rejuvenated Castle of Mey has gradually mirrored the Queen Mother's affection for it. Its very inaccessibility is part of its attraction, and despite a seemingly vulnerable position Mey radiates a great sense of permanence, and defiance of its solitude and oppressive climate. The Queen Mother's decision to buy the most northerly castle in Britain – a decision which many people found hard to understand – has been clearly vindicated, and it is to be hoped that the allure of this most improbable but most delightful of Royal homes will continue to enchant her successors.

Looking out from the garden on the west side of the castle to the huge skies over the Pentland Firth; in the far distance, the Orkneys

INDEX